CENTRAL GOVERNMENT BUDGETS IN INDIA

An Analysis

About the Author

S.P. Ganguly, retired from the Indian Audit and Accounts Service at the end of 1985. He retired from the post of Commissioner-cum-Secretary, Finance Department, Government of Tripura, while holding the rank of Accountant-General in the Indian Audit and Accounts Department.

This book has, therefore, behind it the experience of a person who was responsible for the formulation of budget of a state, in addition to his intimate knowledge of budget, finance and accounts, as a member of the Indian Audit and Accounts Service. His other book, *Fundamentals of Government Budgeting in India* received laudable comments from the then Comptroller and Auditor General of India.

CENTRAL GOVERNMENT BUDGETS IN INDIA

An Analysis

(Second Revised and Enlarged Edition)

S.P. GANGULY
Ex-Chairman, Pay Commission
Mizoram

CONCEPT PUBLISHING COMPANY, NEW DELHI 110059

ISBN 81-7022-824-7

Second Revised and Enlarged Edition 2000

Published and Printed by

Ashok Kumar Mittal
Concept Publishing Company
A/15-16, Commercial Block, Mohan Garden
NEW DELHI 110059 (India)

Phones : 5648039, 5649024
Fax : 5648053
Email : *publishing@conceptpub.com*

PREFACE

(To the First Edition)

The analysis of the figures of Budget and Accounts of the Central Government in this book is a simple analysis and not an economist's analysis. However, a chapter has been added in this book on economic and functional classification of Central Government Budget.

I shall regard my labour fruitful if this book is useful to the readers in appreciating the financial problems and policies of the Central Government in proper perspective.

Shri Rochila Saiawi, IA&AS, has kindly gone through the manuscripts of this book and made some suggestions. I am grateful to him for this assistance.

Aizawl — S.P. GANGULY

PREFACE

(To the Second Revised Edition)

The book has been updated with the latest figures available, mainly from the Report on Currency and Finance of the Reserve Bank of India for 1997-98.

Calcutta
19.1.2000

S.P. GANGULY

ACKNOWLEDGEMENTS

List of books and documents consulted

1. Budget documents of the Central Government
2. Reserve Bank of India's Reports on Currency and Finance
3. Economic and Functional Classification of Central Government Budgets
4. Economic Survey of the Government of India of different years
5. The Great Depression of 1990, Dr. Ravi Batra
6. "Development Digest", October 1971, Dr. Mahbub-ul-Haq
7. "Games FMs Play" by D.H. Pai Panandikar, *Hindustan Times*, Delhi, 27 March, 1990.
8. Fundamentals of Government Budgeting in India – First Edition (1987)

CONTENTS

PART I – INTRODUCTORY

Chapters

I	:	General
II	:	Structure of Budget

I

GENERAL

Budgeting and accounting are integral parts of our daily life. Nevertheless, most of us are overawed with the words "Budget" and "Accounts".

2.1 Budgeting, in simple words, is an estimation of resources and application of those resources for some desired purposes. Budgeting is necessary not only for an individual or Government, but this is also necessary for all aspects of human activities. It is common knowledge that budgeting is necessary for commercial activities. Even for exploitation of natural resources there should be proper budgeting. For example, in the absence of proper budgeting our export of iron ores for earning foreign exchange is an easy way at present may result in our mortgaging the future to such an extent that for utilizing the increased capacity of our steel production we may have to import iron ores in future. Again, in the absence of any national budgeting for use of forest resources, we are already on the brink of a national calamity, in the form of environmental imbalances and pollution, due to over-use of (rather depredation) our forest resources. For avoidance of another such disaster, immediate attention is necessary for national budgeting for our water resources.

2.2 When there is budgeting, it has to be followed by accounting. While budgeting is an estimation or forecast of availability of resources and their application, accounts, kept separately, show to what extent the resources were actually available and how those resources were really applied for different desired purposes.

In the morning when a person gets up, he plans how he will utilise the day; this is budgeting of his available time of 24 hours in that day. Similarly, when a person goes to the market with the money in his pocket, he mentally plans what are the things and how much of each he would purchase with the money that he has got with him. This is budgeting. Again, after the purchases are made, he calculates how much he has spent in the market; this is accounting. Taking into account the balance he has brought back and the money available in the house he calculates how much he is left with for the remaining days of the month and how he will utilise the same for different purposes and to what extent, keeping in view the progress of expenditure till then; this is financial planning. These are very mundane examples of how we do our budgeting, accounting and financial planning in our daily lives. These are very important for an individual's daily life. Only with such budgeting, accounting and planning, it will be possible for him to put his time and money to the best use.

2.3 Similarly, for a Government also budgeting, accounting and financial planning are necessary not only for the administrative needs but also for welfare of the people in its broadest sense. Government budget, however, is not merely estimation of its receipts and expenditures. In preparing this vital document, Government treats it as an annual financial plan and uses it as a vital tool for meeting administrative needs and securing socio-economic goals in the best possible public interest.

3. Earlier, Government budgeting used to be confined to financial budgeting only, as the activities of Government were mostly confined to administrative activities, and law and order responsibilities. With ever increasing emphasis on developmental activities, now, budgeting for achieving physical targets within a time frame, with the finances provided for in the budget, has assumed great importance. As a result, when financial outlays are provided for any development scheme in the budget, simultaneously, physical targets are also laid down for achieving the same with the financial provision within a time frame. This is necessary as any extra time for achieving the fixed physical targets means more expenditure in the form of cost escalation. As such, the estimation for physical targets to be achieved within a time frame with the money provided for in the budget is absolutely essential. This estimation or budgeting of physical targets related to the financial outlay is "Performance Budget", which enables Government to keep watch not only on progress of expenditure with reference to the financial budget but also review the actual performance in the ground, as compared to the money spent, to find out whether value for money has been obtained.

4. In my book "Fundamentals of Government Budgeting in India" an attempt had been made to briefly explain the structure of Government budget, different stages of preparation of Government budget, what the Annual Financial Statement (Budget), and its accompanying documents contain, the relation between budget and accounts etc. indicating relevant provisions of the Constitution, wherever necessary. The present book is intended to indicate how over the years, the resources have actually

been raised and how the same have been applied.

5. At the beginning of each year, budget is the most important document as the resources have to be raised to the extent indicated therein and these are to be applied for the desired purposes and to the extent indicated in the budget. When, however, the financial year is over, the accounts reflect the actual implementation of the financial planning for the relevant year shown in the budget. In fact, after the accounts are prepared, original budget figures are relevant, in the main, for finding out how far the estimates prepared at the beginning of the year were correct, the extent of deviations in raising resources and in their application and regularisation of expenditure in excess of budget provision (including supplementary provision, if any, obtained during the course of the financial year). The accounts figures speak for themselves, much more than verbose explanations, to those who are able to read the accounts. Prudent financial planners, therefore, take their lessons from the accounts figures. But the lesson drawn from accounts figures differ from person to person depending on individual perception. As such my attempt would be to present the accounts figures (figures of budget estimate for the year for which accounts figures are not ready) in the proper perspective so that the readers are able to draw their own conclusions.

II

STRUCTURE OF BUDGET

6. Before initiating any discussions on budgetary transactions over the years, it would be appropriate to discuss the structure of the Annual Financial Statement (which is actually the budget) mentioned in Article 112 of the Constitution of India for the Central Government and Article 202 of the Constitution of India for the State Governments. The structure of budget is indicated below:

A. Consolidated Fund

All revenues received by Government, all loans raised by Government by issue of treasury bills, loans or ways and means of advances and all moneys received by Government in repayment of loans from the Consolidated Fund vide Article 266(1) of the Constitution of India.

Consolidated Funds

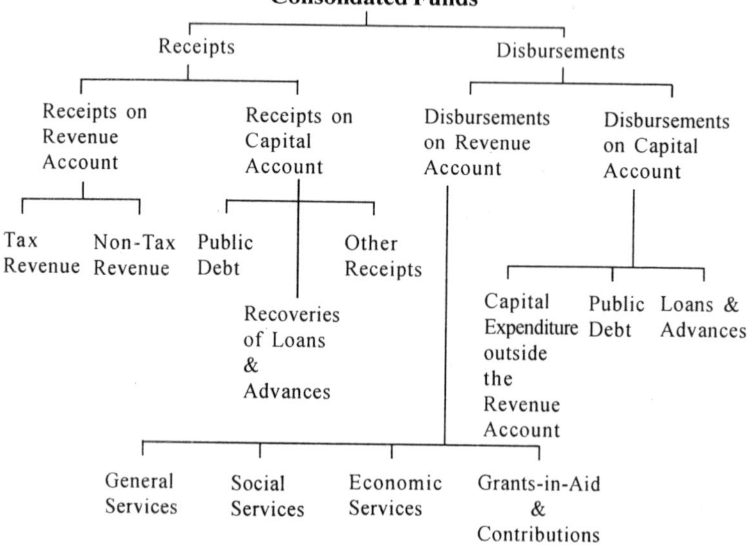

B. Contingency Fund

Contingency Fund may be established, by law, under Article 267 of the Constitution of India into which such sums, as may be determined by such law, are paid from time to time and the said funds is placed at the disposal of the President or the Governor of a state, as the case may be, to enable advances to be made by him out of such fund for the purposes of meeting unforeseen expenditure pending authorisation of such expenditure by Parliament or the State Legislature by law.

Contingency Fund

- Receipts
- Disbursements

C. Public Account

All other public moneys received by or on behalf of Government are credited to the Public Account under Article 266(2) of the Constitution of India.

Public Account

- Receipts
  - National Small Savings Fund
  - State Provident Fund and other Accounts
  - Reserve Funds
  - Deposits and Advances
  - Suspense and Miscellaneous
  - Remittances
- Disbursements
  - National Savings Fund
  - State Provident Fund and other Accounts
  - Reserve Funds
  - Deposits and Advances
  - Suspense and Miscellaneous
  - Remittances

7.1 Receipts on Revenue Account — Receipts on Revenue Accounts are divided into:
(i) Tax Revenue
(ii) Non-Tax Revenue

7.2 Tax Revenue — Tax Revenue includes 'Taxes on Income and Expenditure' (Corporation tax, taxes on income other than corporation tax etc.), 'Taxes on Property and Capital Transactions'

(Estate Duty, Taxes on Wealth, Gift Tax etc.), 'Taxes on Commodities and Services' (Customs Duty, Union Excise Duty, etc.)

7.3 Non -Tax Revenue

Non-Tax Revenue includes 'Fiscal Services' (currency, coinage and mints etc.), 'Interest Receipts, Dividends and Profits (Receipts on account of interest on sums lent, Dividends and Profits from investments, etc.) and 'Other Non-Tax Revenues' in the shape of receipts of different individual departments and also grants-in-aid and Contributions (External grant assistance, Aid Materials, etc.).

8. Disbursements on Revenue Account

Disbursements on Revenue Accounts are broadly on General Services (Organs of State, Fiscal Services, Interest Payment and Servicing of Debt, Administrative Services, Pensions and Miscellaneous General Services and Defence Services), Social Services (Education, Sports and Youth Services, Art and Culture, Medical and Public Health, Family Welfare, Water Supply and Sanitation, Housing, etc.), Economic Services (Agriculture and Allied Activities, Rural Development, Special Area Programme, Irrigation and Flood Control, Energy, Industry and Minerals, Transport, Communication, Science and Technology), and Grants and Contributions (Grants-in-Aid to States and Union Territory Governments, Payment of States' share of Union Excise Duties, Technical and Economic Co-operation with other countries, etc.).

9. Revenue Surplus/ Deficit

The difference between the Revenue Receipts and Revenue Disbursements is the Revenue Surplus (if the Revenue Receipts exceed the Revenue Expenditure) or Revenue Deficits (if the Revenue Disbursements exceed the Revenue Receipts).

10. Receipts on Capital Account

The Receipts on Capital Account include mainly Public Debt comprising Internal Debt and External Debt (in the case of Central Government only), Recoveries of Loans and Advances (from State Governments, Union Territory Governments and in the case of Central Government recoveries of loans and advances from Foreign Governments also).

11. **Total Consolidated Fund Receipts** The Receipts on Revenue Account (or Revenue Receipts) and the Receipts on Capital Account together constitute the "Total Consolidated Fund Receipts".

12. **Disbursements on Capital Account** The divisions of disbursements under Capital Account are the same as those under Revenue Account Disbursements. In addition, the disbursements under Capital account include the section 'Public Debt' providing for repayment of Market Loans, Treasury Bills, External Debts (in the case of Central Government only) etc. and payment of loans and advances to State Governments, Foreign Governments, Public Sector undertakings, etc.

13. **Total Consolidated Fund Disbursement** The total of the "Disbursements-Revenue Account" and "Disbursements-Capital Account" is "The Total Consolidated Fund of India–Disbursements".

14. In the Budget, only the net figure, if any, under Contingency Fund is taken into account.

15. **Receipts under Public Account** The receipts under Public Account include National Small Savings Funds, State Provident Fund and Other Accounts, Reserve Funds, Deposits and Advances, Suspense and Miscellaneous and Remittances.

16. **Disbursement under Public Account** The disbursement under Public Account are under the divisions as in the case of receipts.

17. **Total Receipts of Government** The Total of "Receipts Under Revenue Account", "Receipts Under Capital Account" and "Receipts Under Public Account" is the grand total of Receipts of Government.

18. **Total Disbursement of Government** Similarly, the total of "Disbursements Under Revenue Account", "Disbursements Under Capital Account" and "Disbursements Under Public Account" is the grand total of disbursements of Government.

19. After taking into account the opening cash balance, the difference between total receipts of Government and total disbursements of Government represents its closing cash balance.

PART II – RESOURCES

I

GENERAL

20.1 Resources of Government are collected usually from the following sources:

Revenue Receipts

(i) Tax Revenue

(ii) Non-Tax Revenue including Grants-in-Aid and Contributions

Receipts on Capital Account

(i) Loans raised by Government–both long term and short term.

(ii) Receipts in the shape of recoveries of loans and advances paid by Government.

20.2.1 For the moneys received in Public Account as Small Savings, Provident Funds, Reserve Funds, Deposits and Advances, Government has a liability to repay the same to whom the moneys pertain (i.e. investors in small savings, subscribers to Provident Fund, and Depositors, etc.) or spend the money for specified purposes outside budgetary allocation (moneys in Reserve Funds) whenever necessary.

Substantial balances remain under these heads throughout any financial year, on some of which Government pays interest (e.g. Small Savings, Provident Funds, Deposits bearing interest etc.).

20.2.2 Suspense and Remittance heads in Public Account are of transitory nature. If the correct classification of a transaction is not known, when it occurs, it is temporarily put under suspense, pending adjustment under the correct head after ascertaining the correct classification. A familiar example of Remittance is money order. In principle, there should not be any balance under Suspense or Remittance heads for long. In practice, however, it is usual that a net credit balance under these heads remains throughout a financial year.

20.2.3 Money available in Public Account available for Government Expenditure

Money available in Public Account remain merged with cash balance of Government with its banker, i.e. the Reserve Bank of India and are, therefore, available for expenditure of Government. The funds available in Public Account (i.e. representing the net credit balance) are, therefore, resources of Government like other borrowed funds.

II

REVENUE RECEIPTS

21.1.1 The following are the figures of revenue receipts of the Central Government since 1950-51 at the end of each five-year period up to 1985-86 and thereafter of each year upto 1990-91 (Budget Estimates).

Year	Revenue Receipts (Rupees in crores)(*)	Increase (per cent)
1950-51	405.86	
1955-56	481.19	18.5 (as compared to 1950-51)
1960-61	877.46	82.3 (as compared to 1955-56)
1965-66	2,344.40	167.2 (as compared to 1960-61)
1970-71	3,341.90	42.5 (as compared to 1965-66)
1975-76	8,075.40	141.6 (as compared to 1970-71)
1980-81	12,828.60	58.9 (as compared to 1975-76)
1985-86	29,178.00	125.1 (as compared to 1980-81)
1986-87	34,768.00	20.4
1987-88	38,992.00	12.2
1988-89	45,740.00	17.3
1989-90	54,614.00	19.4
1990-91	57,650.00	5.6
1991-92	69,117.00	19.2
1992-93	77,573.00	10.2
1993-94	79,650.00	2.7
1994-95	95,549.00	20.0
1995-96	1,14,914.00	20.0
1996-97	1,31,686.00	14.6
1997-98 (R.E)	1,45,773.00	10.7
1998-99 (B.E)	1,70,300.00	16.1

R.E– Revised Estimate B.E – Budget Estimate

(*) *Source* : Report on Currency and Finance of the Reserve Bank of India.

21.1.2 It will appear from the above that as compared to 1950-51 (Rs. 405.86 crores), revenue receipts of the Central Government registered a growth 7014 per cent in the three and half decades ending 1985-86 (Rs. 29,187.00 crores). After four decades, the revenue receipts for 1990-91 (Rs. 57,650.00 crores) were 14099 per cent more than that of 1950-51. After four and half decades, in 1995-96, the revenue receipts (Rs. 1,14,914.00 crores) were 28204 per cent more than the same in 1950-51. The revenue receipts of 1996-97 (Rs. 1,31,686.00 crores), 1997-98 R.E.(Rs. 1,45,733.00 crores) and 1998-99 B.E. (Rs. 1,70,300.00 crores) were 32335 per cent, 35805 per cent and 41846 per cent more respectively than the same in 1950-51.

21.1.3 The table of revenue receipts will show that the growth of revenue receipts of the Central Government has not been uniform. As compared to 1950-51 (Rs. 405.86 crores), the growth in the last year of the subsequent five-year period i.e. in 1955-56 (Rs. 481.19 crores) was modest 18.5 per cent. This growth rate increased to 82.3 per cent in 1960-61 (Rs. 877.46 crores) when compared to 1955-56. At the end of the next five-year period in 1965-66 (Rs. 2344.40 crores), the increase in revenue receipts of the Central Government was 167.2 per cent. Thereafter, there was a sharp decline in the increase in revenue receipts in 1970-71 (Rs. 3341.90 crores) which was only 42.5 per cent when compared to the revenue receipts of 1965-66. The growth rate of revenue receipts increased to 141.6 per cent in the last year of the next five-year period i.e. in 1975-76 (Rs. 8075.40 crores) when compared to the revenue receipts in 1970-71. In the last year of the next five-year period ending 1980-81 (Rs. 12828.60 crores), the increase in revenue receipts was 58.9 per cent as compared to the revenue receipts of 1975-76. The revenue receipts of 1985-86, which was the last year of the next five-year period, increased by 125.1 per cent when compared to the revenue receipts of 1980-81. Again, while the annual rate of growth of revenue receipts of the Central Government in 1986-87 (Rs. 34768.0 crores) was 20.4 per cent over those in 1985-86, the increase in 1987-88 (Rs. 38992.0 crores) was only 12.2 per cent as compared to 1986-87. The revenue receipts of 1988-89 (Rs. 45740.00 crores) were 17.3 per cent more than the revenue receipts of 1987-88, while the same for 1989-90 (Rs. 54614.00 crores) was 19.4 per cent higher than the revenue receipts of 1988-89. The revenue receipts for 1990-91 (Rs. 57650.0 crores) was only 5.6 per cent more than the same of 1989-90. The revenue receipts of the next five years from 1991-92 to 1995-96 were 19.2 per cent, 10.2 per cent, 2.7 per cent, 19.9 per cent, and 20.0 per cent higher respectively as compared to the revenue receipts of preceding year of each; the lowest growth rate was in 1993-94. The revenue receipts of 1996-97, 1997-98 (R.E) and 1998-99 (B.E) were 14.6 per cent, 10.7 per cent and 16.1 per cent higher respectively as compared to the revenue receipts of the preceding each year.

22.1.1 Revenue Receipts as Tax revenue and non-tax revenue

The break up of the revenue receipts as tax revenue and non-tax revenue is given below for each year shown in paragraph 21.1.1 during the period from 1950-51 to 1990-91.

(Rs. in crores)

Year	Total Revenue receipts	Total Tax revenue	As percentage of total revenue receipts	Total non-tax revenue	As percentage of Total revenue receipts
1	2(*)	3(*)	4	5(*)	6
1950-51	405.86	357.00	88.0	48.86	12.0
1955-56	481.19	411.47	85.5	69.72	14.5
1960-61	877.46	730.14	83.2	147.32	16.8
1965-66	2344.40	1784.60	76.1	559.80	23.9
1970-71	3341.90	2451.30	73.3	890.60	26.7
1975-76	8075.40	6009.80	74.4	2065.60	25.6
1980-81	12828.60	9387.80	73.2	3440.80	26.8
1985-86	29178.00	21140.00	72.4	8038.00	27.6
1986-87	34768.00	24318.00	69.9	10450.00	30.1
1987-88	38992.00	28015.00	71.8	10977.00	28.2
1988-89	45740.00	33751.00	73.8	11989.00	26.2
1989-90	54614.00	38349.00	70.2	16265.00	29.8
1990-91	57650.00	42978.00	74.5	14672.00	25.5
1991-92	69117.00	50069.00	72.4	19048.00	27.6

(Contd.)

1	2(*)	3(*)	4	5(*)	6
1992-93	77573.00	54044.00	69.8	23529.00	30.2
1993-94	79650.00	53449.00	67.1	26201.00	32.9
1994-95	95549.00	67454.00	70.6	28095.00	29.4
1995-96	1,14,914.00	81939.00	70.8	32975.00	29.2
1996-97	1,31,686.00	93701.00	71.2	37985.00	28.8
1997-98(RE)	1,45,773.00	99158.00	67.9	46615.00	32.1
1998-99(BE)	1,70,300.00	1,16,857.00	68.6	53443.00	31.4

(*) *Source*: Reports on Currency and Finance of the Reserve Bank of India.

It will appear from the above that the tax revenue is the major portion (between 67.1 per cent and 88 per cent) of the total revenue receipts of the Central Government, while non-tax revenue varied between 12.0 per cent and 30.8 per cent of the total revenue receipts. However, while the tax revenue has shown a declining trend since 1950-51,and the non-tax revenue has shown upward trend, when compared as percentage of total revenue receipts.

In the three and half decades from 1950-51 (Rs. 357.0 crores) to 1985-86 (Rs. 21,180.0 crores), tax revenue increased by 5833 per cent, while non-tax revenue increased by 15677 per cent from a very modest figure of Rs. 48.86 crores in 1950-51 to Rs. 7704.0 crores in 1985-86. At the end of four decades from 1950-51, in 1990-91 the tax revenue (Rs. 42978.0 crores) was 11939 per cent more than that of 1950-51, while non-tax revenue (Rs.14672.0 crores) had increased by 29843 per cent as compared to that of 1950-51. In 1995-96, i.e., at the end of four and half decades from 1950-51 the tax revenue (Rs. 81939.0 crores) had increased by 23132 per cent, while the increase for non-tax revenue was 67196 per cent. As compared to 1950-51, the increases in 1996-97, 1997-98 (R.E) and 1998-99 (B.E) for tax revenue were 26147 per cent, 27675 per cent and 32633 per cent respectively, while the same for non-tax revenue were 77439 per cent, 97033 per cent and 108967 per cent respectively. The tax revenue (Rs. 42978.00 crores) for 1990-91 was 11939,per cent more than that of 1950-51, while the non-tax revenue (Rs.14672.00 crores) for 1990-91 was 29843 per cent more than that of 1950-51.

22.1.2 Growth of Tax revenue and non-tax revenue

In the four decades and half between 1950-51 and 1995-96 and the four following years, the rates of growth of tax revenue and non-tax revenue have been as follows:

Year	Rate of growth of tax revenue (per cent)	Rate of growth of non-tax revenue (per cent)
1955-56 (as compared to 1950-51)	15.1	42.9
1960-61 (as compared to 1955-56)	77.6	111.4
1965-66 (as compared to 1960-61)	144.4	280.9
1970-71 (as compared to 1965-66)	37.4	59.9
1975-76 (as compared to 1970-71)	145.2	132.0
1980-81 (as compared to 1975-76)	56.2	66.5
1985-86 (as compared to 1980-81)	125.6	123.9
1990-91 (as compared to 1985-86)	103.3	82.5
1995-96 (as compared to 1990-91)	90.7	124.8
1996-97 (as compared to 1995-96)	14.4	15.2
1997-98 (RE) (as compared to 1996-97)	5.8	22.7
1998-99 (BE) (as compared to 1997-98 R.E.)	17.8	14.6

Non-tax revenue

23.1.1 Growth of non-tax revenue

In the year 1950-51, the non-tax revenue of Rs.48.86 crores was merely 12 per cent of the total revenue receipts. By 1955-56, non-tax revenue increased to Rs.67.72 crores registering a growth of 42.9 per cent over that in 1950-51. The tax revenue in 1955-56 was, however only 15.1 per cent more than that in 1950-51. By 1960-61, the non-tax revenue increased to Rs.85.5 crores which was 111.4 per cent more than that in 1955-56. The increase in tax revenue in that period was 77.6 per cent. As compared to 1960-61, non-tax revenue in 1965-66 was 280.9 per cent more. In 1965-66, the tax revenue was 144.4 per cent more than 1960-61. The tax revenue in 1970-71 was merely 37.4 per cent more than that in 1965-66. The non-tax revenue in 1970-71 was only 59.9 per cent more than that in 1965-66. It will thus be noticed that there was a total decline in growth of total revenue receipts at the end of this five year period. As compared to 1970-71, the non-tax revenue was 132.0 per cent more in 1975-76, while in that year the tax revenue was 145.2 per cent more than that in 1970-71. In this five year period, therefore, the growth rate of tax revenue was little more than the non-tax revenue. This position was reversed again in 1980-81, when non-tax revenue was 66.5 per cent more than that in 1975-76, while tax revenue in 1980-81 was 56.2 per cent more than that in 1975-76. In 1985-86, again non-tax revenue was 123.9 per cent more than that in 1980-81, but the increase in tax revenue was 125.6 per cent which was marginally more than that of non-tax revenue. In 1990-91, the tax revenue was 103.3 per cent more than that in 1985-86, while the increase in non-tax revenue during that period 82.5 per cent; there was fall in the rate of growth during the 5 year period ending 1990-91 as compared to that in the preceding 5 year period ending 1985-86. In the next 5 year period ending 1995-96, the increase in tax revenue was 90.7 per cent, while the increase in non-tax revenue was 124.8 per cent as compared to 1990-91. It will be noticed that in the 5 year period ending 1995-96, there was a further fall in the growth rate of tax revenue, but there was substantial increase in the growth rate of non-tax revenue.

In 1996-97, the increase in tax revenue and non-tax revenue as compared to 1995-96 were 14.4 per cent and 15.2 per cent respectively. In 1997-98 (R.E), the rate of increase of tax revenue and non-tax revenue were 5.8 per cent and 22.7 per cent respectively as compared to 1996-97. In 1998-99 (B.E) tax revenue and non-tax revenue increased by 17.8 per cent and 14.6 per cent respectively as compared to

1997-98 (R.E).

23.1.2 One of the reasons for apparent increases in the figures of non-tax revenue, except in the budget estimate for 1990-91, was the growth of interest receipts as indicated below:

Year	Interest receipts	Total non-tax revenue	Interest receipts as percentage of total non-tax revenue
	(Rs. crores)	(Rs. crores)	
	1(*)	2(*)	3(*)
1965-66	306	560	55.0
1970-71	575	891	64.5
1973-74	735	1178	62.4
1974-75	775	1460	53.1
1975-76	934	2066	45.2
1976-77	1105	2172	50.9
1977-78	1441	2732	52.7
1978-79	1427	2672	53.4
1979-80	1360	2772	49.1
1980-81	1795	3441	52.2
1981-82	2215	4001	55.4
1982-83	2852	5035	56.4
1983-84	2668	5016	53.2
1984-85	3963	6690	55.2
1985-86	4586	7704	59.5
1986-87	5339	10450	50.6
1987-88	5745	10977	52.3
1988-89	6973	11989	58.7
1989-90	8466	16265	52.0
1990-91	8730	14672	59.6
1991-92	10933	19031	57.4
1992-93	12488	23529	53.1
1993-94	15062	26201	57.5
1994-95	15797	28095	56.2
1995-96	18419	32975	55.9
1996-97	22106	37985	58.2
1997-98(R.E)	25327	46615	54.3
1998-99(B.E)	27954	53443	52.3

(*)Source : Reports on Currency and Finance of Reserve Bank of India

As compared to 1965-66, the interest receipts in 1985-86, i.e. after two decades, were about 1399 per cent higher. During the next decade ending 1995-96, the interest receipts increased by 302 per cent as compared to 1985-86. However, as compared to 1965-66 the increase in the three decades ending 1995-96 was 5919 per cent. As compared to 1995-96, the increase in interest receipts during 1996-97, 1997-98 (R.E) and 1998-99 (B.E) were 20.0 per cent, 37.5 per cent and 51.8 per cent higher. The increases in interest receipts in the three years ending 1998-99 (B.E) as compared to 1965-66 were 7124 per cent, 8177 per cent and 9037 per cent respectively. During the entire period from 1965-66 to 1998-99 (B.E), the interest receipts were more than 50 per cent of the total non-tax revenue except in 1975-76 and 1979-80.

23.1.3 But the increase in the interest receipts mentioned in the earlier paragraph is, to a large extent, illusory. The loans advanced by the Central Government are from borrowed fund on which it has to pay interest although at a rate lower than the rates of interest charged by it from its borrowers.

The following table shows the liabilities for payment of interest of the Central Government as against its interest receipts during the last two decades ending 1998-99:

(Rupees in crores)

Year	Interest Receipts	Interest Payments	Deficit
1	2	3	4
1978-79	1427	1984	557
1979-80	1360	2292	932
1980-81	1795	2748	953
1981-82	2215	3260	1045
1982-83	2852	4007	1155
1983-84	2668	4869	2201
1984-85	3963	6050	2087
1985-86	4586	7512	2926
1986-87	5339	9237	3898
1987-88	5745	11236	5491
1988-89	6973	14261	7288
1989-90	8466	17735	9269
1990-91	8730	21471	12741

(Contd.)

1	2	3	4
1991-92	10933	26596	15663
1992-93	12488	31075	18587
1993-94	15062	36740	21678
1994-95	15797	44060	28263
1995-96	18419	50045	31626
1996-97	22106	59478	37372
1997-98(R.E)	25327	65700	40373
1998-99(B.E)	27954	75000	47046

The above table shows that in 1978-79, the interest payments exceeded the interest receipts by 39 per cent. After a decade, i.e. 1988-89, the interest payments exceeded the interest receipts by 105 per cent. At the end of the next decade, i.e., in 1998-99 (B.E), the interest payments exceeded the interest receipts by 168 per cent. The table indicates how the debt liabilities of the Central Government have increased over the years involving huge outgo of interest, which is one of the main reasons for the imbalance in its revenue budget, as discussed later.

23.2.1 The public sector enterprises were set up in the core sector with high hopes and at huge investments. But the performance of non-petroleum sector public enterprises has been dismal throughout, although most of them have the advantage of monopoly of their products and, in addition, price preference. Nothing tangible appears to have been done to make the public enterprises remunerative.

The position is really serious. Much of the investments in public sector enterprises is from funds borrowed from foreign sources. The principal and interest on such borrowed funds from foreign sources have to be paid in foreign currency resulting in depletion of foreign exchange reserve. Thus the unremunerative public sector enterprises not only affect the budgetary position of Government, but also cause depletion of the country's foreign exchange reserve. The ideal situation would have been if not only the public sector enterprises were remunerative, but also contributed to country's export efforts or reduction in imports substantially by producing such goods which are otherwise imported and thus adding to or making savings in country's foreign exchange reserve. From the details and discussions which follow it would appear that the high hopes about the public sector enterprises have remained unfulfilled; plausible reasons widely speculated being (i) political interference, (ii) utilisation of public sector enterprises as milch cows by the political masters in power, (iii) over-staffing at the whims of political masters, with connivance of their psychophant bureaucrats, (iv) failure to remove the dead wood in time, (v) irresponsible trade unionism, (vi) failure to upgrade technology and improve efficiency of personnel etc.

23.2.2 Return from investments in public sector undertakings

The main source for augmentation of non-tax revenue should have been the return on the huge investments made in public sector enterprises from borrowed funds, to a large extent from foreign sources. It was stated in the paragraph 5.36 of the Economic Survey for 1973-74 that "In view of the limited potential of additional taxation of the Centre, it is most important that public sector enterprises should make a significant contribution to the growth of public savings." In the Economic Survey for 1980-81 it was observed that "..... the problem of raising adequate resources for the 6th plan can only be solved if adequate returns are earned on large investments made in the public enterprises both at the Centre and the States." In the Economic Survey for 1989-90, it has been stated that "the remunerative commercial activities also have not been generating adequate return flow by way of dividends and interest".

The performance of public sector enterprises of the Centre was far from satisfactory as will be evident from the following table, although there are signs of slow but gradual improvements since 1981-82 (except in 1983-84), thanks to the remunerative oil sector undertakings of the Central Government.

23.2.3 It will appear from the table given below that as measured by net profit to capital employed, the best result of 4.5 per cent was achieved in 1989-90 during the period from 1975-76 to 1989-90. The net profit (after tax) earned in 1989-90 was substantially higher as compared

Year	No. of running public enterprises	Capital Employed	Net Profit (after tax)	Net Profit (after tax) as per cent to capital employed
		(Repees in Crores)		
1	2	3(*)	4(*)	5(*)
1975-76	121	8824	129	1.5
1976-77	149	10887	184	1.7
1977-78	155	12065	91	0.8
1978-79	159	13969	40	0.3
1979-80	169	16182	74	0.5
1980-81	163	18207	203	1.1
1981-82	188	21935	445	2.0
1982-83	193	26526	614	2.3
1983-84	201	29851	240	0.8
1984-85	207	36382	909	2.5
1985-86	211	42965	1172	2..7
1986-87	214	51835	1771	3.4
1987-88	221	55554	2060	3.7
1988-89	226	67619	2994	4.4
1989-90	233	84437	3782	4.5
1990-91	236	102080	2270	2.2

Source : Economic Surveys.

to the previous years. However, out of the total net profit (after tax) of Rs. 3782 crores in 1989-90, the petroleum sector companies contributed Rs. 2900 crores i.e. about 77 per cent of the total. In other words, 200 odd non-petroleum sector public enterprises (almost 90 per cent of the public enterprises) out of the total 222 public enterprises contributed only Rs. 882 crores towards the profit; the ratio of net profit (after tax) to capital employed in respect of the non-petroleum sector public enterprises was only 1.3 per cent in 1989-90. Nevertheless, this was an improvement over 1988-89 when the non-petroleum sector public enterprises contributed only Rs. 471 crores. It is, however, clear that there is urgent need for improvement of the performance of non-petroleum sector public enterprises.

23.2.4 As a result of the poor performance of the public sector enterprises in the non-petroleum sector, the contribution of the public sector enterprises to the general revenues of the Central Government has been insignificant, as indicated below, despite the massive investments made in them.

23.2.5 The table below shows the contribution of public sector enterprises to the general revenues of the Central Government:

Year	Devidends paid by public sector enterprises to Central Government (excluding dividends from Railways, Post & Telegraph and Reserve Bank of India) *(Rupees in Crores)*	As percentage of total non-tax revenue
	1(*)	2
1970-71	17	1.9
1975-76	37	1.8
1980-81	82	2.4
1984-85	197	2.9
1985-86	205	2.7
1986-87	297	2.8
1987-88	394	3.6
1988-89	265	2.2
1989-90	505	3.0
1990-91	564	3.8

(*) *Source* : Reports on Currency and Finance of the Reserve Bank of India.

23.2.6 The dividends from the public sector enterprises were less than 2 per cent of the total non-tax revenue in 1970-71 and 1975-76 and remained less than 3 per cent in 1980-81 (2.4 per cent), 1984-85 (2.8 per cent), 1985-86 (2.7 per cent) and 1986-87 (2.9 per cent). In 1987-88, the dividends were 3.6 per cent of the total non-tax revenue.

In 1988-89, such dividends declined to 2.2 per cent of the total non-tax revenue. According to the revised estimates of 1989-90, these dividends were estimated to be 3.0 per cent of the total non-tax revenue. The budget estimate of 1990-91 indicated that such dividends would be 3.8 per cent of the total non-tax revenues.

23.3 Incidentally, the position regarding the State Government public sector undertakings is worse. The latest information as on 31st March 1987, only in respect of such undertakings, is available in a report published by the Comptroller and Auditor General of India (State Government Public

Enterprises, Concept Performance and Accountability) published in April 1989. According to this report, there were 843 companies and 76 corporations in the States with an investment of Rs. 44,738 crores. The total investment in the 843 companies in the States was Rs. 11,219 crores (share capital Rs. 3,579 crores and loans Rs.7,640 crores). Of these 843 companies, as on 31st March 1987, 206 had cumulative profits of Rs. 151 crores, 514 had cumulative loss of Rs. 2,020 crores, while the remaining 123 companies were defunct or under liquidation/construction. Thus these companies in the States had cumulative losses amounting to Rs. 1,869 crores as on 31st March 1989.

The financial results of the 76 corporations were not available in the above-mentioned report. The Economic Survey for 1990-91 indicated that the State Electricity Boards incurred losses amounting to Rs. 2,825 crores in 1988-89 and Rs. 3,517 crores in 1989-90. The performance in terms of rate of return on capital was negative, being about (-) 12.8 per cent in 1988-89 and (-) 13 per cent in 1989-90. The State Transport Corporations incurred losses amounting to Rs. 283 crores in 1988-89, which were estimated to be Rs. 359 crores in 1989-90 (pre-actuals).

The losses of the State Public Sector Undertakings mean dependence on the States' finances which ultimately result in more transfers from the Centre to the States adding to the deficits of the Central Government.

23.4.1 Persistent poor performance of the public sector enterprises ultimately resulted in a shift of Government policy towards them. In his speech introducing the final budget for 1991-92, Shri Manmohan Singh, Finance Minister, said; "For the founding fathers of our Republic, a public sector that would be vibrant, modern, competitive and capable of generating large surpluses was a vital element in the strategy of development. The public sector has made an important contribution to the diversification of our industrial economy. But there have been a number of shortcomings. In particular, the public sector has not been able to generate internal surpluses on a large enough scale. At this critical juncture, it has therefore become necessary to take effective measures so as to make the public sector an engine of growth rather than an absorber of national savings without adequate return. This has been widely accepted, but thought and action in this regard are still far apart. To bridge this gap, the portfolio of public sector investments would be reviewed so as to concentrate the future operation of the public sector in areas that are strategic for the nation, require high technology for the economy, and are essential for the infrastructure. In order to raise resources, encourage wider public participation and promote greater accountability, upto 20 per cent of Government equity in selected public sector undertakings would be offered to mutual funds and investment institutions in the public sector, as also to workers in these firms. Public enterprises which are chronically sick and which cannot be turned around, will be referred to the Board for Industrial and Financial Reconstruction (BIFR) or to a similar high powered body to be set up, for formulation of revival or rehabilitation schemes; a social security mechanism will be created to fully protect the interests of the workers likely to be affected by the rehabilitation packages of the B.I.F.R. Autonomy in management, and corresponding accountability, would be provided through a system of memorandums of understanding between the Government and public sector enterprises".

It would thus appear that the new policy was for diluting Government investment in the public sector undertakings, instead of serious efforts to make them strong, cost-effective and viable organisations capable of generating resources for strengthening the national economy. This sudden reversal of the entire philosophy behind setting up of the public sector undertakings was shocking to many right thinking votaries of a strong public sector and it is no wonder that many of them considered this as an easy way of raising some resources through disinvestments of shares of public sector enterprises and thereby reduce pressure on budget. In fact, this disinvestment process started in 1990-91, when it was proposed to disinvest equity holdings in public sector enterprises to the extent of Rs. 2500 crores; no disinvestment, however, took place in that year.

23.4.2 The Economic Survey for 1991-92 (Part II) observed as follows in paragraph 2.86:

" The public sector will continue to perform an important role in the coming years.

(i) The role envisaged for it would mainly be in areas where investment is of an infrastructural nature and where private participation is not forthcoming to an adequate extent within a reasonable time. Thus, the public sector will continue to play a dominant role in areas like energy, transport, communications and irrigation. However, if private initiative comes forward to participate in creating such infrastructure on reasonable terms, including full protection of people's interest, such initiatives would be encouraged.

(ii) The public sector would play a useful role in augmenting basic resources of the country like land, forest, water, ecology and science & technology. The public sector will have responsibility for meeting social needs and for regulation of long-term interests of the society like population control, health, education, etc.

(iii) In large parts of its operations where commodities or services are produced and distributed, the principle of market would be applied as basic operating guideline, unless it is necessary to protect the interests of the poorest in the society. This implies recovery of costs and efficiency in operations.

In the above role assigned to the public enterprises there is marked deviation from the existing role played so far by these enterprises, which allowed virtual monopoly and, in addition, price preference."

23.4.3 The Economic Survey for 1991-92 (Part II) further observed as follows (paragraph 2.99):

"As the proposed reduction in fiscal deficit involves a substantial cut in the budgetary support, it is necessary that public enterprises are able to generate internal surpluses, on a substantial scale. Fiscal discipline is, therefore, necessary on the part of state and Central public undertakings to hasten the process of fiscal correction....."

23.4.4 The Economic Survey for 1995-96 stated as follows (paragraph 19 to 21 Part 7):

"The Industrial Policy Statement announced by Government in July 1991 envisaged disinvestment of a part of Government holdings in the share capital of selected Public Sector Enterprises (PSEs) in order to provide market discipline and to improve the performance of public enterprises. A total amount of around Rs. 10,500 crores has already been disinvested to the public sector financial institutions, mutual funds and general public.

To protect the interests of workers, and provide a social safety net for labour a National Renewal Fund (NRF) was set up in February 1992 and schemes have been proposed to assist the employees in re-training, redeployment and counselling. Provision of funds through NRF also exist for cases where workers retire voluntarily or are declared surplus. To implement the NRF schemes an empowered authority has been created. An amount of Rs. 542.29 crores was released from NRF during 1993-94 and Rs. 261.13 crores during 1994-95. An estimated 75000 workers had opted for voluntary retirement under the scheme. A major portion of the amount has been utilised in the textiles sector.

The provisions of SICA was extended to public sector undertakings in December 1992......."

23.4.5 The performance of the public sector enterprises after the change of the policy mentioned above was as follows:

Year	No of running public enterprises	Capital employed (Rs. crores)	Net profit (after tax) (Rs. crores)	Net profit (after tax) as per cent of capital employed
1992-93	237	139930	3400	2.4
1993-94	240	159840	4550	2.8
1994-95	241	162450	7190	4.4
1995-96	239	173990	9570	5.5
1996-97	236	202020	10260	5.1

Source : Economic Survey, 1998-99.

From the above table it will appear that after the change in policy in 1991-92, in the following two years, 1992-93 and 1993-94, the performance of the public sector enterprises deteriorated as compared to 1986-87, 1987-88, 1988-89 and 1989-90. From 1994-95, however, there was improvement. The best performance was in 1995-96 when net profit as per cent of capital employed was 5.5 per cent. No doubt, the net profit has increased steadily, but this has to be measured with reference to the capital employed. Presumably, because of the steady increases in net profits of public sector enterprises, the Reserve Bank of India in its Report on Currency and Finance, 1997-98, Vol. I, stated that "...... the performance of public sector enterprises improved considerably during the recent years". It is, however, perhaps debatable whether even the highest return of 5.5 per cent (net profit) as a per cent (net profit as per cent of capital employed) is adequate or satisfactory when Central Government raises funds at almost double that rate as interest.

23.4.6 The following table shows the contribution of the public sector enterprises to the general revenues of the Central Government, after the change in policy about them in 1991-92:

Year	Devidends paid by public sector enterprises to Central Government (excluding dividends from Railways, Post & Telegraph and Reserve Bank of India) *(Rupees in Crores)*	As percentage of total non-tax revenue
1991-92	708	3.7
1992-93	992	4.2
1993-94	948	3.6
1994-95	1215	4.3
1995-96	1748	5.3
1996-97	2355	6.2
1997-98 (R.E)	2362	5.1
1998-99 (B.E)	3173	5.9

23.4.7 The Economic Survey for 1998-99 stated as` follows, indicating that the policy of disinvestment has been continuing and would continue (paragraphs 18 and 19 in Part 7):

"In the Union Budget 1998-99, disinvestment in Public Sector Enterprises (PSEs) namely, GAIL, VSNL, CONCOR and IOC was announced. The CONCOR issue was introduced in the market in November 1998 and raised

Rs.221.65 crores. It was also announced that Government holding in Indian Airlines would be brought down to forty- nine per cent over the coming three years. To underscore the Government's commitment to privatisation, the Budget also indicated that in the majority of cases, Government shareholding in Public Sector Enterprises will be brought down to twenty-six per cent. However, the Government will continue to retain majority holding in PSEs involving strategic considerations.

The Disinvestment Commission has so far submitted eight reports covering forty-three PSUs. In its last report submitted in August 1998, the Commission has made specific recommendations for Air India Ltd. and Central Electronics Ltd. suggesting strategic sale for the former and deferment of disinvestment in the latter. Ten more PSUs have been referred to the Commission in November 1998. The Commission has undertaken diagnostic studies in respect of these undertakings for giving recommendations".

23.4.8 It may be mentioned in this connection that while presenting the budget for 1999-2000, Shri Yashwant Sinha, Minister of Finance stated as follows:

"Government's strategy towards public sector enterprises will continue to encompass a judicious mix of strengthening strategic units, privatising non-strategic ones through gradual disinvestment or strategies sale and divising viable rehabilitation strategic for weak units.

The disinvestment programme of the Government draws primarily upon the recommendations of the disinvestment Commission........."

Tax Revenue

24.1.1 Direct taxes and Indirect taxes

The broad divisions of tax revenue are direct taxes and indirect taxes. Direct taxes are (i) Income tax, (ii) Corporation tax, (iii) Wealth tax, (iv) Gift tax etc. Indirect taxes are (i) Central Excise Duty, (ii) Sales tax, (iii) Entertainment tax, (iv) Duties on imports or exports of goods or services. Broadly speaking, while the direct taxes are realised directly by the Government from the assessees on their income, property etc., indirect taxes are realised through intermediaries like producers, sellers, importers, exporters etc., the effect of which is finally passed on to the ultimate consumer. As mentioned in paragraph 24.1 of my book "Fundamentals of Government Budgeting in India", taxes are imposed by Government for utilising the resources thus collected for common good of the people. Philosophy behind such taxation is that society itself should pay for its development. Taxation, however, should not be such as to burden an individual beyond his capacity to pay, making it oppressive. That would be against our aim for establishing a welfare society. Ideal taxation system should ensure that its burden is equitably distributed amongst payers on the basis of capacity for payment. This equity is established by making persons similarly situated to pay equal amount of tax (horizontal equity) and at the same time ensuring that those who are better placed economically share a greater burden of tax (vertical equity).

24.1.2 Receipts under direct taxes and indirect taxes

Receipts under direct taxes and indirect taxes were as follows during 1950-51 to 1998-99 (B.E):

Year	Direct taxes (Rs. Crores)	Per cent of tax revenue	Indirect taxes (Rs. Crores)	Per cent of tax revenue
1	2(*)	3	4(*)	5
1950-51	129.51	36.4	227.49	63.6
1955-56	115.78	28.2	295.69	71.8
1960-61	205.46	28.1	524.68	71.9
1965-66	474.00	26.5	1311.00	73.9
1970-71	511.00	20.9	1940.00	79.1
1975-76	1480.00	24.6	4530.00	75.4
1980-81	1992.00	21.2	7396.00	78.8
1985-86	3574.00	18.3	16894.00	81.7
1986-87	4065.00	17.1	19689.00	82.9
1987-88	4157.00	15.2	23193.00	84.8
1988-89	6074.00	18.0	27677.00	82.0
1989-90	6081.00	15.9	32268.00	84.1
1990-91	6903.00	16.3	36075.00	83.7

(Contd.)

1	2(*)	3	4(*)	5
1991-92	10,248.00	20.5	39821.00	79.5
1992-93	12,074.00	22.4	41970.00	77.6
1993-94	12,522.00	23.4	40937.00	76.6
1994-95	18,409.00	27.3	49045.00	72.7
1995-96	22,288.00	27.2	59651.00	72.8
1996-97	25,375.00	27.1	68326.00	72.9
1997-98 (RE)	30,145.00	30.4	69013.00	69.6
1998-99 (BE)	34,910.00	29.9	81947.00	70.1

(*) Source : Reports on Currency and Finance of the Reserve Bank of India.

24.1.3 As compared to 1950-51, the direct taxes increased by almost 59 per cent by 1960-61, while the indirect taxes increased by almost 131 per cent. During the next decade ending 1970-71, the direct taxes increased by 149 per cent as compared to 1960-61, while the indirect taxes increased by almost 270 per cent. By 1980-81, direct taxes increased by 290 per cent and indirect taxes by 281 per cent as compared to 1970-71. In the following decade ending 1990-91, direct taxes rose by 247 per cent, while indirect taxes rose by 388 per cent as compared to 1980-81. In 1998-99 (B.E), the direct taxes were 406 per cent more than the same in 1990-91, while the increase in indirect taxes was 127 per cent during that period. It will thus appear that except for the decade ending 1980-81, when the rise in direct taxes was slightly more than indirect taxes, the rise in direct taxes was lower than indirect taxes till 1990-91. The position was reversed thereafter; the rise in indirect taxes became gradually lower, with corresponding rise in direct taxes.

24.1.4 The share of direct taxes to the total tax revenue has declined gradually from 36.4 per cent in 1950-51 to 15.2 per cent in 1987-88. It increased to 18.0 per cent in 1988-89. The share of tax revenue was 15.9 per cent in 1988-89 and 16.3 per cent in 1990-91. Thereafter, the share of tax revenue gradually rose to 30.4 per cent in 1997-98 (R.E); there was a slight fall in 1998-99 (B.E), when it was 29.9 per cent. On the other hand, the share of indirect taxes in total tax revenue had increased from 63.6 per cent in 1950-51 to 84.8 per cent in 1987-88. The share of indirect taxes in 1988-89, 1989-90 and 1990-91 was 82.0, 84.1 and 83.7 per cent respectively. Thereafter, with the gradual rise in the share of direct taxes, the share of indirect taxes came down to 69.6 per cent in 1997-98 (R.E); there was a slight rise in 1998-99 (B.E), when it was 70.1 per cent.

24.2.1 Direct taxes affect only a small section of the population which is affluent, while the tentacles of most of the indirect taxes affect the entire population, rich or poor, who use the goods or services. Thus the poor has also to share the indirect tax, except that on luxury goods out of the reach of the poor, equally with the affluent members of society. This negates the principle of equity which stipulates that those who are better placed should bear a greater burden to tax. Even the indirect tax on a luxury good may affect the poor although he may not consume it. For example, increase in indirect tax on petroleum product increases the cost of production or availability of other goods and services of common use which are needed by even the poorer section of the people. Nevertheless, Central Government has been dependent on the soft option of increasing tax revenue mostly through indirect taxes which do not directly affect the people, but do so indirectly in the shape of increased cost of goods and services. In other words, this is an attempt to placate ordinary people who constitute the vote bank for the political parties, so that they do not directly feel the pinch of an indirect tax which they do not have to pay directly to Government, being unaware of its spiralling effect on prices of goods and services which they use and on which they really pay tax in the shape of enhanced cost for them. It is high time that a fresh look is taken at this method of increased dependence on indirect tax, which has perhaps reached the oppressive level for the poor.

24.2.2 The over-dependence on indirect taxation has been the subject matter of serious consideration from time to time, without, however, any remedy. The following observations were made in this matter in the Economic Survey for the year 1971-72.

"But certain problems still persist. The rapid increase in

commodity taxation vis-a-vis taxation of incomes and wealth has been a major feature of the fiscal developments during the past two decades. Whereas the revenue from taxation of incomes and wealth has risen fractionally from 2.4 per cent of national income in 1950-51 to 3.0 per cent in 1970-71, the revenue from indirect taxes has increased as a proportion of national income from 4.2 per cent to 11.0 per cent, or nearly threefold. This was perhaps inevitable, since widening the base of direct taxes in a country consisting overwhelmingly of poor people has inherent limitations. But the comparative lack of progressiveness in indirect taxes has to be constantly guarded against". (Paragraph 11.9 of the Economic Survey, 1971-72).

This matter was again discussed in the Economic Survey for 1973-74 as follows:

"An important feature of Indian fiscal system is the heavy reliance that has traditionally been placed on indirect taxes, particularly excise duties, for raising revenue. Indirect taxes today account for about 80 per cent of the total tax revenue of the Centre as against 70 per cent in 1962-63. This heavy reliance on indirect taxes has been subject of considerable criticism both in Parliament as well as among fiscal experts. However, agricultural income is not subject to Central income tax and also because of administrative difficulties involved in collecting direct taxes, the heavy emphasis on indirect taxes is perhaps inevitable. At the same time, it has to be recognised that indirect taxes must not be inherently regressive as is sometimes supposed. A well conceived structure of indirect taxes can be an effective means for mopping up a part of the high incomes earned by relatively well-to-do sections of society. Through a careful choice of taxable commodities and of rates of commodity taxation, it is possible to impart a considerable element of progression to the system of indirect taxation". (Paragraph 5.32– Economic Survey, 1973-74). It further states as follows :

"Taking all factors into account, it would appear that the potentialities of commodity taxation have by no means been exhausted. There is, for example considerable scope for using excise duties to curb consumption of luxury and semiluxury items, mopping up excess profits in the case of commodities in short supply and for encouraging exports. However, the untapped potential is not as large as is sometimes assumed". (Paragraph 5.35 of the Economic Survey, 1973-74).

However, in 1977-78 an attempt was made to put more emphasis on raising additional revenue through direct taxes than indirect taxes, as mentioned in paragraph 5.11 of the Economic Survey for 1977-78 quoted below:

"In the field of taxation, the 1977-78 Central Budget shows a significant departure from the previous budgets. Unlike in the past when the bulk of the revenue from additional taxation was raised from taxation on commodities, the current year's budget relied more on direct taxes. Out of a total additional tax revenue of Rs. 126.6 crores, as much as Rs. 88.3 crores or 70 per cent was to be raised from changes in the rates of income and wealth tax. "But the efforts of 1977-78 were not lasting ones as will be evident from the following observations in the Economic Survey for 1979-80:

"The tax proposals in 1979-80 Budget reflect some of the basic weaknesses in the Indian Tax structure. The direct tax base, which does not include agricultural income, is very restricted and efforts to raise additional tax revenue have to rely on indirect taxes. While it is possible to tax luxury consumption heavily the base for such taxes is quite small and the required resources cannot be raised from this source alone. As a result, additional levies necessarily fall on items which enter into common consumption...........

Our ninety per cent of the additional tax revenue was raised from indirect taxes". (Paragraph 5.14 of Economic Survey, 1979-80).

24.3.1 In his speech (paragraph 65) presenting the final budget for 1991-92, Sri Manmohan Singh, the then Finance Minister had said:

"The revenue from direct taxes, both as a proportion of GDP and as a percentage of total tax revenues, has registered a steady decline over time. This trend has to be reversed, so as to restore equity in, and balance to our fiscal system. Resources for development must be raised from those who have the capacity to pay. For this purpose, we must place greater emphasis on direct taxes. This calls for increased rates wherever necessary and a better tax compliance. At the same time, rationalisation of the system, which reduces the maximum marginal rate of tax, simplifies the procedures, reduces the plethora of concessions, and brings the average rates of income-tax at various levels of income to more appropriate levels, is necessary."

As mentioned earlier in paragraphs 24.1.3 and 24.1.4, the share of direct tax to the total tax revenue has been showing increasing trend though marginally, since 1991-92. Although Government is aware that direct tax base is presently restricted, nothing much has yet been done to alter the position. Even in 1998-99 (B.E), the share of indirect tax was 70 per cent of total tax revenue.

24.3.2 The question of taxing the income from agriculture was discussed in the Economic Survey for the year 1971-72 as follows :

"One major area for direct taxation is the income originating in agriculture, which however, comes under the orbit of the states. The difficulties faced by the State Governments to tap adequately the rural sector, besides widening economic disparities, have resulted in an increasing reliance on their part on Union Government's assistance. At the same time, the proportion of land revenue and agricultural income tax collected by the states to national income from agriculture has steadily declined from 1.63 per cent in 1960-61 to 0.85 per cent in 1970-71." (Paragraph 12.0 of the Economic Survey, 1971-72).

In the Economic Survey for 1973-74 it has been observed that agricultural income is not subject to Central income tax. Again, in the Economic Survey for 1979-80 it has been observed that the direct tax base, which does not include agricultural income, is very restricted. It is true that the agricultural income presently does not come under the Central income tax. Under the Constitution of India, it is for the State Governments to tap this source of income for raising resources. So far the States have not done so. This certainly has resulted in more transfer of resources from Centre to the States.

24.3.3 Apart from the spiralling and massive price support given to the agricultural products, heavy subsidies are allowed on agricultural inputs like fertilizers, seeds, irrigation facilities, electricity, etc. For example, the subsidy on fertilizers alone, which was Rs. 60 crores in 1976-77, increased to Rs. 4601 crores (an increase of more than 7568 per cent) in 1989-90.

24.3.4 The following table shows the subsidy on fertilizers paid since 1990-91 :

Year	Indigenous (urea) fertiliser	Imported (urea) fertiliser	Fertiliser subsidy to small and marginal farmers	Sale of decontrolled fertiliser with concessions to farmers	Total
		(Rs. in crores)			
1990-91	3730	659	–	–	4389
1991-92	3500	1300	385	–	5185
1992-93	4800	996	–	–	5796
1993-94	3800	762	–	–	4562
1994-95	4075	1166	–	528	5769
1995-96	4300	1935	–	500	6735
1996-97	4743	1163	–	1672	7578
1997-98	6600	722	–	2596	9918
1998-99 (R.E)	7360	238	–	3790	11388
1999-2000 (B.E)	8000	750	–	4500	13250

Thus it will be seen that in one decade the subsidy on fertilizers has increased by 188 per cent from Rs. 4601 crores in 1980-81 to Rs. 13,250 crores in 1999-2000 (R.E)

24.3.5 Apart from the subsidy mentioned above, the direct investments in successive plans in the agriculture and allied sectors were massive as will be evident from the following table :

	Investment in agriculture and allied sectors including rural development and special area programmes				Investment in Irrigation and Flood Control		
	Total Plan Outlay/ actuals (Rs. crores)	Amt. (Rs. crores)	Increase in % as compared to earlier plan	As % of total outlay/ actual	Amt. (Rs. crores)	Increase in % as compared to earlier Plan	As per cent of total outlay/ actual
1	2*	3*	4	5	6*	7	8
First Plan ('51-56)–actuals	1960	290	–	14.8	434	–	22.1
Second Plan ('56-61)–actuals	4672	549	89.3	11.5	430	1.0	9.00
Third Plan ('61-66)–actuals	8577	1089	98.3	12.7	665	54.7	7.8
Annual Plan ('66-69)–actuals	6625	1107	–	16.7	471	–	7.1
Fourth Plan ('69-74)–actuals	15779	2320	113.0	14.7	1354	103.6	8.6
Fifth Plan ('74-79)–actuals	39426	4865	109.7	12.1	3877	186.3	9.8
1979-80–actuals	12177	1996	–	16.3	1288	–	10.6
Sixth Plan ('80-85)–actuals	109292	15200	212.4	13.8	10930	181.9	9.9
Seventh Plan ('85-90)–actuals at current prices	218729	31510	107.0	14.4	16590	51.8	7.6
Eighth Plan (1992-97)–at 1991-92 prices	434100	63642	102.0	14.7	32525	96.0	7.3
1997-98 annual plan	139626	17224	–	12.3	10638	–	7.6
1998-99 annual plan	105187	9746	–	9.3	375	–	0.3

**Source* : Economic Survey for different years.

24.3.6 Although not commensurate with the massive investment indicated above, Gross Domestic Product in the Agricultural sector (agriculture, Forestry, etc.) at 1980-81 prices showed gradual increase, except slight falls in 1965-66 and 1986-87, as a result of such investment, as will be evident from the following Table:

Year	Gross Domestic Product in Agricultural Sector (Agriculture, Forestry etc.) (Rs. crores)	Increase in per cent
1	2**	3
1950-51	24024	
1955-56	27890	15.2
1960-61	32793	17.6
1965-66	32310	-1.5
1970-71	41385	28.1
1975-76	46183	11.6
1980-81	48536	5.1
1985-86*	56841	17.1
1990-91*	69860	22.9
1995-96*	279204	–
1996-97*	303572	8.9
1997-98 (a)	301436	-0.7

(*) Provisional
(a) Quick estimate
(**) *Source* : Economic Survey

Note : Figures upto 1990-91 are based on 1980-81 prices. Figures from 1995-96 onwards are based on 1993-94 prices.

24.3.7 It will appear from the above that there has been substantial income generation in the agriculture sector. This has created a class of rich farmers, who are no less conspicuous in luxury consumptions than those, say, in the industrial sector. While the marginal and small farmers, or even medium scale farmers having income up to a prescribed level may be left out of the tax net, there appears to be no plausible reasons for not collecting tax from rich framers on their income from agriculture. If the States fail to tap this source of resources, the result ultimately is more transfers of resources from the Centre to the States making them more dependent on the former. As such, if the State Governments do not show the will to tax the rich farmers, it is for the Central Government to initiate appropriate measures so that this source of resources does not remain untapped any longer.

24.4.1 The share of income tax is more than 95 to 99 per cent of the total collection of direct taxes as will be evident from the following table, which shows that during the 5 years ending 1998-99 (B.E), the share of income tax was consistently more than 99 per cent:

Year	Total Direct taxes (Rs. crores)	Total Income tax (Rs. crores)	Income tax as per cent of total direct taxes
1980-81	1992	1905	95.5
1981-82	2763	2662	96.3
1982-83	3004	2888	96.1
1983-84	3325	3198	96.2
1984-85	3562	3423	96.1
1985-86	3780	3612	95.6
1986-87	4065	3878	95.4
1987-88	4157	4046	97.3
1988-89	6074	5940	97.8
1989-90	6081	5890	96.9
1990-91	6903	6666	96.6
1991-92	10248	9930	96.9
1992-93	12074	11596	96.0
1993-94	12522	12363	98.7
1994-95	18409	18288	99.3
1995-96	22288	22202	99.6
1996-97	25375	25287	99.6
1997-98(R.E)	30145	30004	99.5
1998-99(B.E)	34910	34754	99.6

Source: Reports on Currency and Finance of the Reserve Bank of India.

As the income tax level has already reached almost saturation level, it is perhaps necessary to innovate some other sources, apart from agricultural income, for augmentation of the direct tax base. The fact that income tax accounts for more than 99 per cent of direct taxes clearly indicates that such innovation is still lacking.

24.4.2 In an answer to a Parliament question the then Finance Minister had stated on 20th April 1990 that the total arrears and current demand of income tax outstanding at the end of November 1989 was about Rs. 4,62,011 crores which were more than the total estimated receipt of income tax of the Central Government in 1987-88. It is, therefore, necessary to ensure better collection of the tax.

The Economic Survey for 1990-91, in reviewing the deteriorating revenue deficit of Central Government observed that "the shortfall in revenue collections during 1990-91 as compared with the budget estimates, has further accentuated the problem".

24.4.3 In paragraph 2.17 of the Economic Survey for 1991-92 (Part II – Sectoral Developments), it was observed that the "thrust of fiscal management in 1991-92 was to meet the challenges posed by the unparalleled fiscal crisis being faced by country. The budget, *inter alia*, aimed at expenditure reduction and increase in Government income. Measures in the field of direct taxes were targeted at reversing the declining trend in the share of these taxes in total tax revenues and as a proportion of Gross Domestic Product. The objectives of changes in indirect tax regime were: reducing excessive reliance on customs duties for additional resource mobilisation; ensuring price stability for essential commodities and goods; curbing conspicuous consumption; encouraging indigenous industry and improving the competitiveness of the industrial sector, particularly, the export-oriented industries. Accordingly, the overall impact of the proposals in 1991-92 Budget relating to excise and customs duties was revenue negative for the Central Government..........".

24.4.4 In presenting the budget for 1993-94, the then Finance Minister, Manmohan Singh had said as follows (paragraph 51 to 54):

"In framing these proposals I have been acutely conscious of the conflicting requirements of comprehensive reform of the tax structure on the one hand, and the need to protect revenues to finance the large increase in the Plan, on the other. Last year significant reforms were made in personal income taxation based on the recommendations of the Chelliah Committee. Reform of corporate taxation was deferred until the detailed recommendations of the Chelliah Committee were received. These have since been received. The Committee has also recently submitted its final report on indirect taxes, recommending significant reduction in customs duties as well as rationalisation and simplification of excise duties.

I accept the broad thrust of the Chelliah Committee's recommendations on both direct and indirect taxes. We must move as rapidly as possible to a regime of moderate tax rates in direct taxation, which will encourage better compliance especially if supplemented by efforts at broadening of the tax base. We must also move to a regime of low to moderate customs duties which is essential for efficient and competitive industrialisation. Our excise duties should also be simplified with fewer rates and our long term aim should be to move to a Value Added Tax System. However, a nationwide value added tax system cannot be introduced overnight. There has to be a broad agreement among the Centre and the States on the design of such a system. In order to promote informed discussion and debate, I am requesting the National Institute of Public Finance and Policy to prepare the design of a possible value added tax system.

Although all the major recommendations of the Chelliah Committee are important, they cannot be implemented immediately for the simple reason that tax reform, which typically involves lower tax rates collected on a broader base, often involves a loss of revenue in the short run. Fiscal experts tell us that the loss of revenue will be made up in the medium term, but there is no guarantee that this will happen immediately, and Finance Ministers have to look after the short term if they want to survive in the medium term. I hope the House will agree with me that a phased transition is needed.

A key issue in phasing the transition is whether to do a little on all fronts or to make decisive changes in certain areas, with a clear declaration of progress to be made in other areas in future. I have thought over this matter carefully and I feel that decisive action in critical areas is more important than marginal improvements on all fronts. The most critical area for action at present is customs duties. Despite the adjustments in customs duties in the last two budgets, our duties are still much higher than in most of our competitor countries, especially on capital goods. With these duties, and the resulting high capital costs, our producers will never be able to compete in world markets. Nor can we expect new investment, both domestic and foreign, to flow into areas with export markets in view, if high customs duties make them uncompetitive. Yet it is such investments that we need most at present if we want to reduce our dependence on external assistance. We cannot and must not continue with the approach of setting up industries aimed solely at the domestic market in the belief that replacing imports *ipso facto* contributes to self reliance, without considering at what cost we are affecting the replacement. In fact, replacement at unduly high cost contributes to inefficient industrialisation, an inability to export and a permanent dependence on external assistance. We must take a bold initiative in this area while taking due care to protect the legitimate concerns of our industry. Normally, the revenue loss from customs duty reduction could have been made up through higher excise duties. However, there are compelling reasons for rationalising and reducing excise duties over a wide range of industries because many of our duties are too high and parts of industry are also suffering from recessionary conditions."

24.4.5. In presenting the budget for 1995-96 the then Finance Minister Manmohan Singh had stated (paragraphs 47-48):

"Over the past three years, we have made a number of structural changes in our tax laws covering both direct and indirect taxes. Unlike earlier isolated attempts to modify the tax system, these changes were part of a medium term programme of tax reform guided by certain general principles that have gained wide acceptability. We wanted to build a structure which is simple, relies on moderate tax rates but with a wider base and better enforcement, serves the objectives of equity and provides the incentives and signals consistent with developing an internationally competitive, dynamic economy.

Direct taxation is the most equitable form of raising revenues, but our experience in the earlier years of high tax rates showed that high rates did not lead to high collections. I am happy to report that our decision to reduce rates and thereby encourage compliance has yielded good results. Personal income and corporation taxes, taken together, are expected to increase by more than 25 per cent in 1994-95. The share of direct taxes in GDP has increased from 2.1 per cent in 1990-91 to 2.8 per cent in 1994-95."

24.4.6 The Economic Survey for 1998-99 observed as follows (paragraph 5) :

"The budget for 1998-99 carried the process of tax reforms further by widening the tax base in the case of personal income tax and by introducing major procedural simplifications...... ".

24.4.7 In paragraph 53 it has been explained why the figures of accounts have not been compared with the figures of GDP as is done in Economic Survey and Report on Currency and Finance of Reserve Bank of India. But to show what has been effect of tax reforms carried out since 1991, the growth of tax revenue as a per cent of GDP is shown in the table below for the years 1989-90 to 1999-2000 (B.E.).

(Rupees in Crores)

Year	GDP	Total tax Revenue (Gross) (excluding U.T. Taxes)	Tax Revenue as per cent of GDP
1989-90	4,56,821	50,667	11.09
1990-91	5,35,534	56,458	10.54
1991-92	6,16,799	66,096	10.72
1992-93	7,05,918	73,122	10.36
1993-94	8,10,749	74,542	9.19
1994-95	9,63,492	92,093	9.56
1995-96	11,18,964	1,10,978	9.92
1996-97	12,76,974	1,28,484	10.06
1997-98 (Prov.)	14,09,779	1,39,906	9.92
1998-99 (R.E)	15,87,411	1,48,394	9.35
1999-2000 (B.E)	17,85,838	1,67,214	9.36

The above figures speak for themselves.

III

RECEIPTS ON CAPITAL ACCOUNT

25.1.1 Capital Receipts

Receipts on capital account are meant for disbursements on capital account with the object of either creation of durable assets or liquidating recurring liabilities. A durable asset may be productive either directly or indirectly. For example, capital investment on construction of a road reduces cost of transportation apart from serving a social objective of better communication; it is productive indirectly. On the other hand, an investment in setting up of a factory is directly productive. In a developing economy huge capital expenditure is essential for expeditious development. As such, it is not unusual that recourse to borrowing of funds both internally and also from external sources is taken. The purpose of investing the capital receipts for creation of durable assets is that such assets will generate sufficient return on such investments for not only liquidating the liability incurred (including interest liability) in raising the capital receipts, but also will contribute to the revenue resources of the Government. On the other hand, if the capital receipts are utilised for liquidating recurring liabilities, the revenue expenditure for the future years is reduced. To give an example, if capital receipts are utilised for construction of building, it may reduce recurring liability of payment of rent of a building hired by Government for its own requirement. If, however, the building is let out, the rent received adds to the revenue of the Government. But ideally in the first case, the reduction in recurring liability of payment of rent should exceed the amount of repayment liability of the borrowed fund and interest liability thereon. In the second case, the rent earned from the building should exceed the repayment liability of the borrowed funds and interest thereon so that there is net addition to the revenue resources of the Government. In practice, however, the Central Government had even to finance revenue expenditure from capital receipts due to persistent revenue deficits since 1979-80 onwards as discussed in paragraph 27.6.3 to paragraph 28.1.2.

25.1.2 As mentioned earlier in paragraph 10, the receipts on capital account comprise Public Debt and recoveries of loans and advances (paid mostly from borrowed funds). The figures of capital receipts also include the figures of net receipts in Public Account (e.g. net receipts of Small Savings, net credit under State Provident Funds, net receipts of Deposits, net receipts in Reserve Funds, net inter-state settlements, etc.). Receipts on capital account during the period from 1950-51 to 1999-2000 were as follows :

Year	Total Receipts on Capital Account	Increase in per cent
1	2	3
1950-51	105	–
1955-56	281	107.2
1960-61	1,127	301.1
1965-66	1,646	46.5
1970-71	2,524	53.4
1975-76	4,697	86.1
1980-81	9,432	100.8
1985-86	16,708	77.1
1986-87	18,529	10.9
1987-88	22,026	18.9
1988-89	25,673	16.6
1989-90	30,020	16.9
1990-91	38,997	29.9
1991-92	38,528	-1.2
1992-93	36,178	-6.1
1993-94	55,440	25.6
1994-95	68,695	23.9
1995-96	58,338	-14.9
1996-97	61,544	5.5
1997-98 (RE)	96,731	57.2
1998-99 (BE)	1,05,933	9.5

Source : Reports on Currency and Finance of the Reserve Bank of India.

25.1.3 Growth of Capital Receipts — It will appear from the above that as compared to the insignificant amount of Rs. 105 crores as receipts on capital account in the year 1950-51, the receipts on capital account amounting to Rs. 105,933 crores in 1998-99 (B.E) was 1000 times more. But there is no consistency in the growth of receipts on capital account. Besides, the receipts on capital account were less as compared to the respective preceding year, in 1991-92, 1992-93 and 1995-96.

25.2.1 Debt and Other Liabilities of Central Govt. — The capital receipts mentioned in paragraph 25.1.2 resulted in enormous increase of debt and other liabilities of the Central Government as will be evident from the following table :

As at the end of	External Debt		Internal Liabilities		Total Internal liabilities	Total Debt and other liabilities
			Internal Debt	Other liabilities		
1	2		3	4	5	6
1951	32		2,022	811	2,833	2,865
1961	782		3,974	2147	6,121	6,903
1971	6,485		7,663	5716	13,379	19,864
1981	11,298	(13479)#	30,864	17187	48,451	59,749
1982	12,328	(15445)#	35,653	20204	55,857	68,185
1983	13,682	(17577)#	46,939	13682	71,190	84,872
1984	15,120	(20214)#	50,264	29877	80,141	95,261
1985	16,637	(24004)#	58.537	38267	96,804	1,13,441
1986	18,153	(26638)#	71,039	48292	1,19,331	1,37,484
1987	20,299	(32312)#	86,312	59935	1,46,247	1,66,546
1988	23,233	(36578)#	98,646	73692	1,72,338	1,95,561
1989	25,746	(46838)#	1,14,498	89527	2,04,025	2,29,771
1990	28,343	(54100)#	1,33,193	106656	2,39,849	2,68,192
1991	31,525	(66017)#	1,54,004	129029	2,83,033	3,14,558

The figures in brackets indicate the outstanding external debt at year-end exchange rate.

Source : Economic Survey for defferent years.

25.2.2 Growth of external debt of Central Government — As compared to the outstanding external debt of only Rs. 32 crores in 1950-51, the same was at the end of 31st March 1990, 80,356 per cent more and stood at Rs. 28,343 crores. External debt was estimated Rs. 31,525 crores at the end of March 1991. As will be evident from the figures in brackets shown in the above table, the real liability is much more.

25.2.3 Growth of internal liabilities — The internal liabilities had also shot up from Rs. 2833 crores at the end of March 1951 to Rs. 2,39,849 crores as at the end of March 1990 (increase of 8366 per cent). The internal liabilities rose further to Rs. 2,83,033 crores at the end of March 1991.

25.2.4 Total debt and other liabilities — The total debt and other liabilities of the Central Government increased from Rs. 2865 crores as at the end of March 1951 to Rs. 2,68,192 crores at the end of March 1990 (an increase of 9261 per cent). The total debt and other obligations were Rs. 3,14,558 crores at the end of March 1991. If the outstanding external debt is converted at the year end exchange rate, the total debt and other liabilities would be much more.

25.2.5 The rates of growth of external debt and internal liabilities were as follows upto the end of March 1991:

As at the end of March	External debt (Rs. Crores)	Rate of growth in per cent	Internal liabilities (Rs. crores)	Rate of growth in per cent
1	2*	3	4*	5
1951	32	–	2,833	–
1961 (As compared to March 1951)	782	2,344	6,121	116
1971 (As compared to March 1961)	6,485	2,022	13,379	118
1981 (As compared to 1971)	11,298	74	48,451	262
1982	12,328	9	55,857	15
1983	13,682	11	71,190	27
1984	15,120	11	80,141	13
1985	16,637	10	96,804	21
1986	18,153	9	1,19,331	23
1987	20,299	12	1,46,247	23
1988	23,233	15	1,72,338	18
1989	25,746	11	2,04,025	18
1990	28,343	10	2,39,849	17
1991	31,525	12	2,83,033	18

(*) *Source* : Economic Survey for different years.

25.2.6 It will appear from the above that out of the three decades ending 1980-81, in terms of percentage the rate of growth (2344 per cent) was highest in the decade ending 1960-61 because of the low base of foreign debt (Rs. 32 crores) at the end of 1950-51. The country needed more foreign debts for its plans. In the decade ending 1970-71, the foreign debt increased from Rs. 782 crores at the end of 1960-61 to Rs. 6485 crores at the end of 1970-71. But in terms of percentage the rate of growth in this decade was slightly lower (2022 per cent) than the earlier decade because of the higher base at the end of 1960-61. In the decade ending 1980-81, the foreign debt rose further from Rs. 6485 crores to Rs. 11,298 crores; an increase of 74 per cent.

In the decade ending 1960-61, average annual growth works out to more than 234 per cent. In the subsequent decade ending 1970-71, the average annual growth rate was more than 202 per cent. But in the decade ending 1980-81, the average annual growth sharply declined to 7.4 per cent. It will also appear from the above table that annual rate of growth in each of the subsequent years from 1981-82 to 1990-91 varied between 9 and 15 per cent.

25.2.7 In the case of internal liabilities in the decade ending 1960-61, there was an increase from Rs. 2833 crores at the end of 1950-51 to Rs. 6,121 crores at the end of 1960-61; the growth was 116 per cent. In the decade ending 1970-71, the growth was 118 per cent from Rs. 6,121 crores at the end of 1960-61 to Rs. 13,379 crores at the end of 1970-71. The decade ending 1980-81 recorded a growth of 262 per cent; the increase was from Rs. 13,379 crores at the end of 1970-71 to Rs. 48,451 crores at the end of 1980-81.

In the decade ending 1960-61, the average annual rate of growth of internal liabilities, was 11.6 per cent and in the subsequent decade ending 1970-71 this rate was 11.8 per cent. But there was a sharp increase in the annual average rate of growth of internal liabilities in the decade ending 1980-81; the rate was 26.2 per cent. The above table also shows that the annual rate of growth during the years 1981-82 to 1990-91 varied between 13 and 27 per cent.

25.2.8 In the preceding paragraphs 25.2.1 to 25.2.7 the position of debt and other liabilities of the Central Government upto the year ending March 1991, i.e. prior to financial reforms, has been discussed. The following table shows the position of Debt and other liabilities as at the end of March 1992 to March 2000 (B.E):

(Rs. in Crores)

At the end of	External Debt	Internal Liabilities		Total Internal liabilities	Total Debt and other liabilities
		Internal Debt	Other liabilities		
1	2	3	4	5	6
1992	36,948	1,72,750	1,44,964	3,17,714	3,54,662
1993	42,269	1,99,100	1,60,554	3,59,654	4,01,923
1994	47,345	2,45,712	1,84,911	4,30,623	4,77,968
1995	50,929	2,66,467	2,21,215	4,87,682	5,38,611
1996	51,249	3,07,869	2,47,115	5,54,984	6,06,233
1997	54,238	3,44,476	2,76,962	6,21,438	6,75,676
1998	55,332	3,88,997	3,33,964	7,22,961	7,78,293
1999 (RE)	55,960	4,58,843	3,61,122	8,19,965	8,75,925
2000 (BE)	56,134	7,09,302	2,25,127	9,34,429	9,90,563

Sources 1. Economic Surveys.
2. Receipt Budget, 1999-2000 for the last three years.

25.2.9 The outstanding external debt as at the end of 1998-99 (R.E) amounting to Rs. 55,960.00 crores was 77.5 per cent more than the outstanding amount as at the end of 1990-91 (Rs. 31,525.00 crores). The outstanding external debt at the end of March 2000 is estimated to be Rs. 56,134.00 crores which would be 78 per cent more than that at the end of 1990-91. The figures of external debt are based on historical rates of exchange and would be much more, if calculated at the year end exchange rates.

25.2.10 The internal liabilities (Rs. 8,19,965.00 crores) at the end of 1998-99 (R.E.) was 189.7 per cent more than the outstanding amount (Rs. 2,83,033.00 crores) as at the end of 1990-91. The internal liabilities (Rs. 9,34,429.00 crores) estimated at the end of 1999-2000 would be 230.1 per cent more than the outstanding amount as at the end of 1990-91.

25.2.11 The total debt and other liabilities as at the end of 1998-99 (R.E) amounting to Rs. 875,925.00 crores was 178.5 per cent more than the outstanding amount as at the end of

1990-91 (Rs. 3,14,558.00 crores). The estimated outstanding amount (Rs. 9,90,563.00 crores) of debt and other liabilities at the end of 1999-2000 would be 214.9 per cent more than the outstanding amount as at the end of 1990-91.

25.2.12 The rates of growth of external debt and internal liabilities were as follows as at the end of March 1992 to March 2000 (B.E):

As at the end of March	External Debt	Rate of growth in per cent	Internal liabilities	Rate of growth in per cent
1992	36,948	17.5	3,17,714	12.3
1993	42,269	14.9	3,59,654	13.2
1994	47,345	12.0	4,30,623	19.7
1995	50,929	7.6	4,87,682	13.3
1996	51,249	0.6	5,54,984	13.8
1997	54,238	5.8	6,21,438	12.0
1998	55,332	2.0	7,22,961	16.3
1999 (RE)	55,960	1.1	8,19,965	13.4
2000 (BE)	56,134	0.3	9,34,429	13.9

25.2.13 In the three years ending March 1992, March 1993 and March 1994, the annual growth rate of external debt showed a declining trend from 17.5 per cent to 14.9 per cent and then to 12.0 per cent. In the year ending March 1995, the growth rate declined to 7.6 per cent. The growth rate of external debt fell sharply to 0.6 per cent in the year ending March 1996. In the year ending March 1997, the growth rate increased to 5.8 per cent. In the next three years ending March 2000 (B.E.), the growth rates of external debt were 2.0 per cent, 1.1 per cent and 0.3 per cent respectively. A distinct declining trend is noticed in the growth of external debt since 1991-92, after financial reforms were started.

25.2.14 The growth rate of internal liabilities during the period from 1991-92 to 1999-2000 (B.E) varied between 12.3 per cent and 19.7 per cent. In fact, except for the two years ending March 1994 and March 1998, when the growth rate of interest liabilities was 19.7 and 16.3 per cent respectively, the growth rate during the above period varied between 12.3 per cent and 13.9 per cent. These growth rates are lower than the same in the earlier years ending March 1982 to March 1991. In other words, after the financial reforms started, a declining trend is noticed in the growth of internal liabilities also.

25.2.15 The following table shows the position of debt and other liabilities as per cent of G.D.P :

Year	Internal liabilities	External debt	Total outstanding liabilities
1980-81	35.6	8.3	43.9
1990-91	52.9	5.9	58.8
1991-92	51.5	6.0	57.5
1992-93	51.0	6.0	57.0
1993-94	53.8	5.9	59.7
1994-95	47.0	4.9	51.9
1995-96	45.6	4.2	49.8
1996-97	44.1	3.8	47.9
1997-98 (RE)	45.9	3.5	49.4
1998-99 (B.E)	45.8	3.2	49.4

Source : Economic Survey.

25.3.1 Although, of late, there is a decline in the rate of growth of debts and other liabilities of the Central Government, there is no denying the fact that the total debt and other liabilities of the Central Government have increased enormously over the years involving heavy burden of repayment liabilities of both principal and interest.

In the case of foreign debt both principal and interest are to be repaid in foreign exchange which strain the balance of payments position of the country. Besides, the country has reached a position in which a major portion of the borrowed funds has to be utilised for repayment of earlier debt and interest thereon.

Payment of interest on both foreign debt and internal liabilities affects the revenue budget of the Government. It is true that the Central Government also earns interest by relending the borrowed funds. But net liability has risen enormously because of the massive increase in interest liability as mentioned in paragraph 27.4.2.

On the other hand, the return from the investments has also been inadequate, as has been pointed out from time to time in the annual Economic Survey presented by Government to Parliament for each financial year, a few of which have been quoted in paragraph 23.2.1.

While mounting interest burden increases the revenue expenditure which is an element for revenue deficits since 1979-80, the borrowed funds are used for meeting such deficits adding to the interest burden on the revenue budget. This aspect has been discussed in details in paragraph 27.4.1.

25.3.2 In the Economic Survey for 1989-90, the following observations were made about the debt and other liabilities of the Central Government.

"Internal liabilities, as a whole, have witnessed a significant rise over the years. Thus the ratio of outstanding internal liabilities to GDP increased from 35.7 per cent at the end of 1980-81 to as much as 51.9 per cent at the end of 1988-89 and is estimated to be about 54 per cent by the end of 1989-90. A significant feature has been the sharp increase in other internal liabilities during this period. The ratio of outstanding other internal liabilities to GDP shot up from 12.9 per cent at the end of 1980-81 to 22.6 per cent at the end of 1988-89 and is expected to rise further to 23.5 per cent by the end of 1989-90. These liabilities attract relatively higher interest rates and as such have added to the growing interest liability.

The outstanding external liabilities on Government account have been shown on the basis of historical exchange rates. These liabilities as a ratio of GDP have tended to decline over the years from 8.3 per cent at the end of 1980-81 to 6.5 per cent by the end of 1988-89. The ratio is expected to remain at 6.5 per cent by the end of 1989-90.......... the outstanding external liabilities when computed at the year end exchange rates, showed a rising trend. The ratio of converted external liabilities to GDP increased from 9.9 per cent at the end of 1980-81 to 12.0 per cent at the end of 1988-89.

The total outstanding liabilities of Central Government comprising internal liability and external liability (expressed on the basis of historical exchange rates) have continued to rise over the eighties. These liabilities formed about 44 per cent of GDP at the end of 1980-81 and the ratio increased to over 60 per cent by the end of 1989-90. Taking external liabilities as converted by year end exchange rates, the total outstanding liabilities grew from 45.6 per cent of GDP at the end of 1980-81 to 63.9 per cent at the end of 1988-89.

The growth of Government debt has led to a substantial increase in gross interest payments which have gone up from 11.6 per cent of total Central Government expenditure in 1980-81 to around 14 per cent in 1985-86 and over 19 per cent in 1989-90 (BE). Equally disturbing is the rise in the share of net (of interest receipts) interest payments from 3.6 per cent in 1980-81 to 5.5 per cent in 1985-86 and 10.1 per cent in 1989-90".

25.3.3 In the Economic Survey for 1990-91, a review of the Government's debt position and its implications has been given, which is as follows:

"Internal liabilities as a whole have increased from Rs. 48,451 crores in 1980-81 to Rs. 2,79,528 crores in 1990-91 (R.E.), nearly a six-fold increase in a span of just ten years. The ratio of outstanding internal liabilities to GDP increased from 35.6 per cent in 1980-81 to as much as 54.4 per cent at the end of 1990-91. Among the internal liabilities, other internal liabilities have witnessed a sharp increase as compared with market borrowings. The ratio of outstanding other internal liabilities to GDP shot up from 12.9 per cent at the end of 1980-81 to 24.1 per cent at the end of 1989-90 and has risen further to 25.0 per cent at the end of 1990-91 (R.E.). These liabilities attract relatively higher interest rates and hence, have added to the growing interest payments liabilities.

The outstanding external liability, on the basis of historical exchange rates, as ratio of GDP has tended to decline over the years from 8.3 per cent at the end of 1980-81 to 6.4 per cent at the end of 1990-91 (R.E.). However, the outstanding external liability, when converted at year-end exchange rates, showed a rising trend. The ratio of external liability at year-end exchange rates to GDP increased from 9.9 per cent at the end of 1980-81 to 12.9 per cent at the end of 1990-91.

Total outstanding liabilities of Central Government comprising internal liability and external liability have continued to rise sharply over the 1980's. These liabilities formed about 44 per cent of GDP in 1980-81 and the ratio has increased to about 61 per cent at the end of 1990-91 (R.E.).

The growth of Government debt has led to a substantial increase in gross interest payments which have gone up from 11.6 per cent of the total Central Government expenditure in 1980-81 to 21.4 per cent by 1990-91 (R.E.). Much more disturbing is the rise in net interest from 3.6 per cent of total expenditure in 1980-81 to 12.1 per cent of 1990-91 (R.E.)".

25.3.4 The debt position of the Government of India has been analysed in the Economic Survey for 1991-92 (paragraphs 2.56 and 2.57 in Part II) as follows:

"Outstanding internal liabilities, as a whole, registered a sharp increase in the eighties, from 35.6 per cent of GDP in 1980-81 to 52.2 per cent in 1991-92 (BE). The bulk of this increase was on account of a sharp increase in other internal liabilities (small savings, provident funds etc.) vis-a-vis market borrowings. The share of this category in total internal liabilities increased from 36.3 per cent in 1980-81 to 46.7 per cent in 1991-92 (BE).

As the internal liabilities carry higher rates of interest, this has also contributed in growing interest liabilities."

"The outstanding external liabilities (at historical exchange rates) as a ratio of GDP started declining in the late eighties. The estimated outstanding external liabilities at the end of 1991-92 stood at 5.8 per cent of GDP compared with 8.3 per cent in 1980-81. However, this trend become worrisome when the external liabilities are expressed in terms of year-end exchange rates. The ratio of external liabilities of Central Government at year-end exchange rates to GDP, increased from 9.9 per cent at the end of 1980-81 to 12.9 per cent at the end of 1990-91."

The Economic Survey for 1991-92 (Part II) has further observed in paragraph 2.58 as follows:

"As a result of the fiscal correction measures introduced by the Government, the outstanding internal and external liabilities in 1991-92 as ratio of GDP have shown a marginal fall to 58.0 per cent from 58.8 per cent in the previous year. However, this has not helped in reducing the net interest liability on accumulated debt. In 1991-92, it increased by over 2 percentage points of total expenditure. It would, indeed, take a few years before the reduced level of borrowing has a perceptible impact on the growing interest burden of the Government. It is imperative that the Government should pursue the policy of fiscal correction more vigorously in the coming years".

25.3.5 In introducing the budget for the year 1994-95, the then Finance Minister, Manmohan Singh had stated as follows (paragraphs 10 and 11):

"Our external debt, which is a cause of concern, is growing more slowly now. It grew by about $ 6 billion per year on an average in the latter half of the 1980's. In 1990-91, the debt grew by over $ 8 billion. In 1991-92 and 1992-93, the increase averaged only about $ 3 billion. In the first half of 1993-94, external debt has increased by hardly $300 million. Furthermore, the recent increase in debt has been more than offset by the sharp increase in our foreign currency reserves. I would like to assure the house that we shall remain vigilant on this front so that external debt remains within prudent levels. There is no question of India falling into a debt trap. In fact, we propose to respond to the easier payments position by some of the high cost debt we have incurred in the past. Indian companies will be freely permitted to pre-pay past foreign loans.

Honourable Members are aware that some of our external debt is owed to the IMF. We had approached the Fund in our hour of difficulty. Now that our payments situation has improved considerably and our reserves have been rebuilt to comfortable levels, we are in a position to repay to the Fund somewhat ahead of schedule. Repayments of principal and interest amounting to $1.4 billion are due to the Fund in 1994-95. Instead of following the regular schedule of payments, we intend to pre-pay the entire amount at the beginning of the year. This decision to pre-pay in no sense detracts from the excellent relations we have with the Fund which has helped us immensely in our time of need. We will not hesitate to seek financial support again, if conditions warrant......"

25.3.6 The Economic Survey for 1995-96 described the position of debt of the Central Government as follows (paragraphs 16 and 17):

"Government debt consisting of internal and external liabilities fell from 69.7 per cent of GDP in 1993-94 to 67.0 per cent in 1994-95 (RE). Internal liabilities declined from the 53.8 per cent of GDP in 1993-94 to 51.9 per cent of GDP in 1994-95 (RE). The decline in internal liabilities was mainly because of the decrease in internal debt from 30.7 per cent of GDP in 1993-94 to 29.0 per cent in 1994-95 (RE). "Other Internal Liabilities" consisting of Small Savings and Provident Funds etc. registered a smaller decrease from 23.1 per cent of GDP in 1993-94 to 22.9 per cent of GDP in 1994-95 (RE). The share of market borrowing in total interest liabilities, which was 32.4 per cent in 1980-81 and has been declining over the years because of a reduction in the Statutory Liquidity Ratio reached 25.7 per cent in 1993-94. However, the share increased to 26.8 per cent during 1994-95 (RE) because of the incentive provided by market based interest rates on Government securities.

The external liabilities shown in the budget are at the historical rates of exchange. Since the value of rupee has depreciated considerably over the years, the external liabilities expressed at the current year-end rates of exchange are much higher. External liabilities which at the end of year 1994-95 (RE) were Rs. 50,628 crores at historic rates are actually Rs. 142499 crores at the current year-end exchange rates. External outstanding liabilities have shown a declining trend since 1991-92. At 15.1 per cent of GDP in 1994-95 (RE), there was a decline of 2.7 per cent of GDP since 1991-92."

25.3.7 In the Economic Survey for 1998-99, the position of debt of the Central Government was mentioned as below (paragraphs 17 and 18):

"Aggregate internal liabilities of the Central Government are budgeted to increase to Rs. 8,10,911 crores in 1998-99 (B.E.) from Rs. 7,18,299 crores in 1997-98 (RE). This shows a moderation in the growth of internal liabilities from 15.6 per cent in 1997-98 (RE) to 12.9 per cent in 1998-99 (BE).

External liabilities at the book value (i.e. at the historical exchange rates) increased from Rs. 55242 crores in 1997-98 (RE) to Rs. 57295 crores in 1998-99 (BE). The repayment burden of the debt stock is better reflected by revaluing the debt stock at the current exchange rates at the end of the relevant financial year. When this is done, external liabilities as a proportion of GDP turn out to be much higher than that at historical rates."

26.1 In such a situation, the question of putting a ceiling on borrowing by the Central Government envisaged in Article 292 of the Constitution of India gains more importance. The then Finance Minister Prof. Madhu Dandavate raised this point when he made a statement in the Parliament on 29 March 1990 (paragraph 25.2.2) as reported in the '*Hindustan Times*' (Delhi) of 30 March 1990. But the point remains that since the adoption of the Constitution of India, successive Comptroller and Auditor General of India has been pointing out in each Audit Report on Central Government for each year that Parliament has not fixed any limit on the borrowings of the Central Government under Article 292 of the Constitution of India. Apparently, no notice of the observation of the Comptroller and Auditor General was taken. In paragraph 9.6.2 of my book "*Fundamentals of Government Budgeting in India*" (published in 1987) also it has been mentioned that no limit has been laid down on borrowings of either the Central Government or of any State Government under Articles 292 and 293 respectively of the Constitution of India. It has also been mentioned in that book that while there is a check on the borrowings of the State Governments as no State Government indebted to the Central Government (there is no State Government which is not indebted to the Central Government) can borrow without the approval of the Central Government, there is no check on the borrowings of the Central Government in the absence of any limit laid down by Parliament under Article 292 of the Constitution.

26.2 It may be mentioned here that as a measure of self-discipline on the part of Central Government, Shri Manmohan Singh, the then Finance Minister made the following announcement (paragraph 13 of the Budget Speech), while presenting the budget for 1994-95:

"Turning to the need to strengthen fiscal discipline, I have long felt that Government should not be able to finance its deficits by creating money, through unlimited recourse to the Reserve Bank, by issue of ad hoc Treasury Bills. This practice has also weakened the Reserve Bank's capacity to conduct effective monetary policy. As a corrective measure, I propose to phase out the Government's access to ad hoc Treasury Bills over a period of three years. In 1994-95 the budget deficit is being limited to about two-third of one per cent of expected GDP, or Rs. 6,000 crores. Normally, net issue of ad hoc Treasury Bills for the year as a whole should not exceed this amount. It has also been agreed with the Reserve Bank that the net issue of ad hoc Treasury Bills should not exceed Rs. 9,000 crores for more than ten continuous working days at any time during the year. If this happens, the Reserve Bank will automatically sell Treasury Bills in the market to reduce the level of ad hoc Treasury Bills. This is a historic step which will in due course contribute to a significant improvement in fiscal and monetary discipline and give the Reserve Bank greater scope for effective monetary management. In subsequent years, the recourse to ad hoc Treasury Bills will be progressively reduced and by 1997-98, the Government will cease to have direct recourse to the Reserve Bank for financing its deficit and will have to meet its entire requirements through borrowing from the market."

Consequently, the Reserve Bank of India, in its Report on Currency and Finance for 1994-95, reported as follows:

"One of the major development of 1994-95 pertains to the delinking of budget deficit from automatic monetisation. This was the direct result of the fundamental reform announced in the Union Budget 1994-95 and the historic agreement between the Government and the Reserve Bank of India effected on September 9, 1994 to delink 'The automatic monetisation of budget deficit' by means of ad hoc Treasury Bills and its gradual phasing out by 1996-97...........".

PART III – APPLICATION OF RESOURCES

Chapters

I	:	General
II	:	Revenue Expenditure
III	:	Expenditure on Capital Account

I

GENERAL

26.1.1 Revenue expenditure is the current (consumption) expenditure of Government. Prudent financial policy requires that such expenditure should be met from revenue receipts. In fact, most sound financial policy would be to ensure that revenue receipts should not only be sufficient to meet revenue expenditure, but should also leave a surplus, after meeting such expenditure, so that the surplus may be utilised for expenditure on capital account. However, unlike expenditure on capital account no return is expected from revenue expenditure.

26.1.2 On the other hand, as mentioned in paragraph 25.1.1, capital disbursements are made usually from borrowed funds and other resources (net funds available in the Public account) outside the revenue account, with the objects either of creating assets of durable nature or of reducing recurring liabilities. If there is a surplus in revenue account, the same may also be utilised for such capital expenditure.

26.1.3 It is, therefore, important to distinguish revenue expenditure from capital expenditure so that no legitimate charge on revenue is passed on as capital expenditure for being met from capital receipts, which are mostly borrowed funds. This aspect has been very succinctly dealt with by Shri D.H. Panandikar in an article published in the "*Hindustan Times*" (Delhi) of 27 March 1990 in which he has stated as follows:

"The distinction between revenue and capital is vital. You make it every day every time you open your purse or write your cheque. Take the first type of expenditure. You can buy exotic meals at a five star hotel, order elegant suits from Exquisite Tailors, a box of Havana cigars, shoes from Foot Care and so on. At the end of the month you would discover that there are bills which are still unpaid. You rush to your friend and get a temporary loan. That is your budget deficit. Thank God, unlike Government, you do not inflate money supply in the economy.

"There is also the second kind of expenditure. You can buy shares from the stock exchange, a house in the suburbs or a life policy from the L.I.C. At the end of the month you may also find that you are out of pocket. You run to your friend for a little loan. The outcome in both the cases is the same. You have to pamper your friend. But when it comes to repaying the loan, the two situations will be totally different. You spend on consumption and the money vanishes for good. There is no way you can repay the loan. But when you spend to create an asset you need not worry about the repayment. The money will be there when your friend asks."

26.1.4 Yes, the money will be there to make repayment provided the investment is prudently made ensuring adequate return on such investment. In the chapter which will be immediately following this, we will be dealing with the expenditure on consumption when the money vanishes for good, i.e. revenue expenditure. But before going to the next chapter let us decide with which year we will start detailed yearwise analysis of expenditure, as compared to receipts, apart from the analysis at the end of each five/ten years period starting from 1950-51.

26.1.5 The effects of planning were not fully discernible by the time the first two plans were implemented. Besides, the country was still then suffering from resources crunch. The third Plan ended in 1965-66. The country had to fight two wars in 1962 and 1965 by then. Between 1966-67 and 1968-69, there were three annual plans only. The fourth Plan was implemented during the years 1969-70 to 1973-74. In between, the country had to fight another war in 1971 and bear the burden of heavy influx of refugees from erstwhile East Pakistan (now Bangladesh). Besides, natural calamities (floods in some areas and droughts in others in 1971-72 and 1972-73) not only affected food production but also caused additional expenditure on relief measures for the victims of the natural calamities.

The effects of the two preceding crisis years (1971-72 and 1972-73) were still there in 1973-74. Before the country could recover from the effects of the crisis years, it had again severe economic strains in 1974-75 due to various factors, the most important of which were (i) large increase in prices of various petroleum products as well as fertilizers in the beginning of this financial year due to steep rise in prices of imported crude in January 1974 and (ii) unsatisfactory production and procurement of foodgrains. The Economic Survey for 1974-75 described the situation as follows:

"The year 1974-75 has proved to be another crisis year for the economy. The budget for 1974-75 had to be framed in the background of severe inflationary pressures coinciding with highly uncertain outlook for agricultural and industrial output as well as for the balance of payments in the wake of steep increase in oil prices in January 1974". The Economic Survey for 1974-75 further stated that "it was also year of determined action on the part of the Government, demonstrating vividly the basic resilience of our democratic policy in grappling with crisis situations". Government realised that budgetary deficits of 1974-75 would greatly exceed the original estimate of Rs. 126 crores. The Economic Survey for 1974-75 went on to say that "the deterioration in budgetary situation together with the unabated price rise compelled Government to take a series of anti-inflationary measures in July 1974". These measures were promulgation of the following ordinances (subsequently replaced by Acts of Parliament) in July 1974.

(i) The Additional Emoluments (Compulsory Deposit Ordinance, 1974 providing for compulsory deposit of whole of additional wages and salaries and half of additional dearness allowance.

(ii) The Companies (Temporary Restrictions on Dividends) Ordinance, 1974 providing for limiting the after tax profits distributed by companies to 33-1/3 per cent of such profits or to 12 per cent of the face value of the equity shares of the company and the dividend payable on its preference share whichever was less.

(iii) Compulsory (Income Tax Payers) Deposit Scheme, 1974 covering all income tax payers whose aggregate net annual income exceeded Rs. 15,000.

If the earlier four years were crisis years, 1975-76 was the turning point. The Economic Survey for 1975-76 stated as follows:

"With the price level showing a declining trend under the impact of the various anti-inflationary measures taken since July 1974, the fiscal policy as unfolded in the budget for 1975-76 laid greater emphasis on accelerating the rate of growth of the economy, which had been none too satisfactory in the last four years. The overall strategy evolved to achieve this objective was to step up the public sector plan outlay, particularly in the core sectors, such as agriculture, irrigation, fertilizers, power, coal, petroleum and shipping and transport and to stimulate domestic savings and channelise these to investment in the desired fields through an appropriate mix of incentives".

We may, therefore, in the main, confine yearwise analysis of growth of expenditure, as compared to receipts from 1976-77 onwards.

II

REVENUE EXPENDITURE

27.1.1 The growth of revenue expenditure has been as follows over the years:

Year	Total Revenue Expenditure (Rs. Crores)	Increase in total Revenue Expenditure (in per cent)
1	2*	3
1950-51	346.64	–
1955-56	440.74	27.1
1960-61	826.21	87.3
1965-66	2,024.60	145.00
1970-71	3,178.90	57.0
1975-76	7,188.50	126.1
1980-81	14,543.60	102.4
1985-86	34,772.00	136.6
1986-87	42,544.00	22.5
1987-88	48,129.00	10.8
1988-89	56,255.00	16.8
1989-90	66,528.00	18.3
1990-91	76,212.00	14.6
1991-92	85,361.00	12.0
1992-93	96,147.00	12.6
1993-94	1,12,366.00	16.9
1994-95	1,26,578.00	12.6
1995-96	1,44,644.00	14.3
1996-97	1,64,340.00	13.6
1997-98 (RE)	1,89,459.00	15.3
1998-99 (BE)	2,18,368.00	15.1

Source : Reports on Currency and Finance of the Reserve Bank of India.

27.1.2 It will appear from the above table that rates of growth of revenue expenditure during the five yearly periods ending 1955-56, 1960-61, 1965-66, 1970-71, 1975-76, 1980-81 and 1985-86 were 27.1 per cent, 87.3 per cent, 145.0 per cent, 57 per cent, 126.1 per cent, 102.4 per cent, and 136.6 per cent, respectively.

These rates of growth are varied indicating that no method was adopted in planning revenue expenditure. Between 1986-87 and 1990-91 rates of growth of revenue expenditure varied between 10.8 per cent (in 1987-88) and 22.5 per cent (in 1986-87). While this was the position in the pre-financial reforms period, the rate of growth of revenue expenditure in the post-financial reforms period between 1991-92 and 1998-99 (BE) varied between 12.0 per cent (in 1991-92) and 16.9 per cent (in 1993-94). The figures for the post-financial reforms period do not indicate any particular concern for curbing revenue expenditure. Such a situation has already developed that no soft options are left. On the other hand, political compulsions have been keeping the successive Governments away from hard decisions.

27.1.3 The rate of growth of revenue expenditure between 1950-51 and 1990-91 as compared to those of revenue receipts were as follows:

Year	Rate of growth of revenue receipts (in per cent)	Rate of growth of revenue receipts exceeded that of revenue expenditure (in per cent)	Rate of growth of revenue expenditure (in per cent)	Rate of growth of revenue expenditure exceeding that of revenue receipts (in per cent)
1	2	3	4	5
1955-56 (as compared to 1950-51)	18.5	–	27.1	46.5
1960-61 (as compared to 1955-56)	82.3	–	87.3	6.0
1965-66 (as compared to 1960-61)	167.3	15.4	145.0	–
1970-71 (as compared to 1965-66)	42.5	–	57.0	34.0
1975-76 (as compared to 1970-71)	141.6	12.3	126.1	--

(Contd.)

1	2	3	4	5
1980-81 (as compared to 1975-76)	58.9	–	102.4	74.0
1985-86 (as compared to 1980-81)	125.1	–	138.6	10.8
1986-87 (as compared to 1985-86)	20.4	–	22.5	10.3
1987-88 (as compared to 1986-87)	12.2	13.0	10.8	–
1988-89 (as compared to 1987-88)	17.3	3.0	16.8	–
1989-90 (RE) (as compared to 1988-89)	19.4	1.0	19.2	–
1990-91 (BE) (as compared to 1989-90 R.E.)	11.2	11.0	10.1	–

27.1.4 It will appear from the above figures that the rates of growth of revenue receipts in the last year of the five-year period ending 1965-66 and 1975-76 were higher by 154 per cent and 12.3 per cent respectively than the corresponding rates of growth of revenue expenditure in those two years. Similarly, in the years 1987-88, 1988-89, 1989-90 (RE), and 1990-91 (BE), the rates of growth of revenue receipts were higher by 13.0, 3.0, 1.0, and 11.0 per cent respectively than the rates of growth of revenue expenditure in those years. On the other hand, in the last year of the five-years periods ending 1955-56, 1960-61, 1970-71, 1980-81 and 1985-86, the rates of growth of revenue expenditure exceeded the rate of growth of revenue receipts by 46.5 per cent, 6 per cent, 34 per cent, 74 per cent, and 10 per cent respectively. The rates of growth of revenue expenditure were substantially higher in the years 1955-56, 1970-71 and 1980-81 (between 34 per cent and 74 per cent). In the year 1986-87 also the rate of growth of revenue expenditure exceeded the same in respect of revenue receipts by 10.3 per cent.

27.1.5 Amongst the five-year period between 1950-51 and 1985-86, the highest growth rate of 167.3 per cent in respect of revenue receipts was in the five-year period ending 1965-66 and in the same five-year period, the rate of growth of revenue expenditure was also the highest, although at a lesser rate than revenue receipts.

27.1.6 The rate of growth of revenue expenditure during the

period 1991-92 and 1998-99 (BE) as compared to those of revenue receipts were as follows:

Year	Rate of growth of revenue receipts (in per cent)	Rate of growth of revenue receipts exceeded that of revenue expenditure (in per cent)	Rate of growth of revenue expenditure (in per cent)	Rate of growth of revenue expenditure exceeded that of revenue receipts (in per cent)
1	2	3	4	5
1991-92 (as compared to 1990-91)	19.2	60.0	12.0	–
1992-93 (as compared to 1991-92)	10.2	–	12.6	23.5
1993-94 (as compared to 1992-93)	2.7	–	16.9	525.9
1994-95 (as compared to 1993-94)	20.0	58.8	12.6	–
1995-96 (as compared to 1994-95)	20.0	39.9	14.3	–
1996-97 (as compared to 1995-96)	14.6	7.4	13.6	–
1997-98 (RE) (as compared to 1996-97)	10.7	–	15.3	43.0
1998-99 (BE) (as compared to 1997-98) (RE)	16.1	6.6	15.1	–

27.1.7 It will appear from the above table that in the first year of the post-financial reforms period, i.e. 1991-92, the rate of growth of revenue receipts exceeded that of revenue expenditure. Thereafter, in 1992-93 and 1993-94, the rate of growth of revenue expenditure exceeded that of revenue receipts by 23.5 per cent and 525.9 per cent respectively. In 1994-95, 1995-96 and 1996-97, the rate of growth of revenue receipts exceeded that of revenue expenditure by 58.8 per cent, 39.9 per cent and 7.4 per cent, respectively. According to 1997-98 (RE), however, the rate of growth of revenue expenditure exceeded that of revenue receipts by 43.0 per cent. The budget estimate for 1998-99 again showed that the growth of revenue receipts exceed that of revenue expenditure by 6.6 per cent.

27.2.1 The growth of revenue expenditure, as compared to revenue receipts in each year during the period 1976-77 to 1990-91 was as follows:

Year	Revenue Expenditure (Rs crore)	Rate of growth (in per cent) as compared to preceding year	Revenue Receipts (Rs crore)	Rate of growth (in per cent) as compared to the preceding year
1975-76	7189	–	8075	–
1976-77	8441	17.4	8753	8.4
1977-78	9362	10.9	9792	11.9
1978-79	10948	16.9	11240	14.8
1979-80	12034	9.9	11340	0.9
1980-81	14544	20.9	12829	13.9
1981-82	15868	8.1	15574	21.4
1982-83	19346	21.9	18091	16.2
1983-84	22890	18.3	20493	13.3
1984-85	27881	21.8	24384	18.9
1985-86	34722	24.5	28884	18.5
1986-87	42544	22.5	34768	20.4
1987-88	48129	10.8	38992	12.2
1988-89	56295	16.8	45740	17.3
1989-90 (RE)	66528	18.3	54614	19.4
1990-91 (BE)	76212	14.6	57650	5.6

Source : Reports on Currency and Finance of the Reserve Bank of India.

27.2.2 It will appear from the above table that in 1976-77, the rate of growth of revenue expenditure (17.4 per cent) was more than that of revenue receipts (8.4 per cent).

The revenue receipts of that year (Rs. 8753 crores) were, however, more than the revenue expenditure. In 1977-78, the rate of growth of revenue receipts (11.9 per cent) was slightly higher than that of revenue expenditure (10.9 per cent). The total revenue receipts of that year (Rs. 9792 crore) were higher than revenue expenditure (Rs. 9362 crore) by Rs. 430 crore. Although in 1978-79, the rate of growth of receipts (14.9 per cent) was less than that of revenue expenditure (16.9 per cent), the revenue receipts

(Rs. 11,240 crores) were more than the revenue expenditure (Rs. 10,948 crores).

27.2.3 Since 1979-80, the revenue expenditure has continued to exceed the revenue receipts causing revenue deficits, although the rate of growth of receipts exceeded that of revenue expenditure in the years 1981-82, 1987-88, 1988-89, 1989-90 and 1990-91. The revenue deficits have been discussed in paragraphs 27.6.3 to 28.1.2. It is interesting to note that the lowest growth rate (0.9 per cent) of revenue receipts was in 1979-80, in which year the revenue deficit was resorted to for the first time at the Centre.

27.2.4 Between 1976-77 and 1990-91, the rate of growth of revenue expenditure varied between 8.1 per cent (1981-82) and 24.5 per cent (1985-86) while that of revenue receipts varied between 0.9 per cent (1979-80) and 21.4 per cent (1981-82). The figures indicate that in 1981-82 an effort was made to augment revenue resources while containing growth of revenue expenditure.

27.2.5 The following table shows the growth of revenue expenditure as compared to the revenue receipts in the post-financial reforms period from 1991-92 to 1998-99 (B.E.):

Year	Revenue Expenditure	Rate of growth of revenue expenditure	Revenue Receipts	Rate of growth of revenue expenditure
1	2	3	4	5
1991-92 (As compared to 1990-91)	85,361	12.0	69,117	19.2
1992-93	96,147	12.6	77,573	10.2
1993-94	1,12,366	16.9	79,650	2.7
1994-95	1,26,578	12.6	95,549	20.0
1995-96	1,44,644	14.3	1,14,914	20.0
1996-97	1,64,340	13.6	1,31,686	14.6
1997-98 (RE)	1,89,459	15.3	1,45,773	10.7
1998-99 (BE)	2,18,368	15.1	1,70,300	16.1

Source : Reports on Currency and Finance of the Reserve Bank of India.

27.2.6 It will appear from the above table that in 1991-92, the rate of growth of revenue receipts (19.2 per cent) was substantially higher than the rate of growth of revenue expenditure (12.0 per cent). In that year, however, revenue expenditure exceeded the revenue receipts by Rs. 16244.0 crores. In 1994-95 also, the growth rate of revenue receipts (20.0 per cent) was higher than that of revenue expenditure (12.6 per cent); the revenue expenditure in that year exceeded the revenue receipts by Rs. 31,029.0 crores. Again in 1995-96, the growth rate of revenue receipts (20.0 per cent) was higher than that of revenue expenditure (14.3 per cent); the revenue expenditure in that year exceeded the revenue receipts by Rs. 29,730 crores. In 1996-97, the growth rate of revenue receipts (14.6 per cent) exceeded that of revenue expenditure (13.6 per cent); the revenue expenditure in that year exceeded the revenue receipts by Rs. 32,654.0 crores. In 1998-99 (B.E) also the rate of growth of revenue receipts (16.1 per cent) was more than that of revenue expenditure (15.1 per cent); the revenue expenditure exceeded the revenue receipts by Rs. 48,068 crores. In the remaining years, i.e., 1992-93, 1993-94 and 1997-98 (RE), the rate of growth of revenue expenditure was more than that of revenue receipts. From these figures it is not evident that any serious attempt was made, as a part of the financial reforms started in July 1991 to contain revenue expenditure and mobilise additional resources so that the revenue receipts exceeded the revenue expenditure. In this connection please see paragraphs 27.5.3 and 27.5.4.

27.3.1 The distribution of revenue expenditure between developmental and non-developmental purposes was as follows :

Year	Total Revenue expenditure (Rs. Cr.)	Revenue expenditure for developmental purpose (Rs. Cr.)	Developmental expenditure as per cent of total revenue expenditure	Revenue expenditure for non-developmental purpose (Rs. Cr.)	Non-developmental expenditure as per cent of total revenue expenditure
1	2*	3*	4	5*	6
1976-77	8411	3162	37.4	5279	62.6

(Contd.)

1	2*	3*	4	5*	6
1977-78	9362	3646	38.9	5716	61.1
1978-79	10948	4512	41.2	6436	58.8
1979-80	12034	5044	41.9	6990	58.1
1980-81	14544	5615	38.6	8929	61.4
1981-82	15868	6524	41.1	9344	58.9
1982-83	19346	7922	40.9	11424	59.1
1983-84	22890	9445	41.2	13445	58.8
1984-85	27881	11909	42.7	15972	57.3
1985-86	34772	14861	42.7	19911	57.3
1986-87	42544	18146	42.6	24398	57.4
1987-88	48129	21198	44.0	26931	56.0
1988-89	56225	24728	44.0	31527	56.0
1989-90	66528	29963	45.4	36565	54.6
1990-91	76212	32239	42.3	43973	57.7

**Source* : Reports on Currency and Finance of the Reserve Bank of India.

It will appear from the above that although the share of revenue expenditure for developmental purposes has increased from 37.4 per cent of the total revenue expenditure in 1976-77 to around 45.4 per cent in 1989-90, the share of non-developmental expenditure continues to be more than that of developmental expenditure. In 1990-91, the share of developmental expenditure again declined to 42.3 per cent of total revenue expenditure.

27.3.2 The following table shows shares of developmental and non-developmental revenue expenditure from 1991-92 to 1998-99 (BE), i.e., in the post-financial reforms period:

Year	Total Revenue expenditure (Rs. Cr.)	Revenue expenditure for developmental purposes (Rs. Cr.)	Developmental expenditure as per cent of total revenue expenditure	Revenue expenditure for non-developmental purposes (Rs. Cr.)	Non-developmental expenditure as per cent of total revenue expenditure
1	2	3	4	5	6
1991-92	85361	35345	41.4	50016	58.6
1992-93	96147	41448	43.1	54699	56.9
1993-94	112366	46061	41.0	66305	59.0
1994-95	126578	51536	40.7	75042	59.3

(Contd.)

1	2	3	4	5	6
1995-96	144644	54350	37.6	90294	62.4
1996-97	164340	60876	37.0	103464	63.0
1997-98 (RE)	189459	70406	37.2	119053	62.8
1998-99 (BE)	218368	82679	37.9	135689	62.1

Source : Reports on Currency and Finance of the Reserve Bank of India.

It will appear from the above table that the share of developmental revenue expenditure to the total revenue expenditure varied between 37.0 per cent and 43.1 per cent. The share of non-developmental revenue expenditure was thus more in the post financial reforms period. In fact, the share of developmental expenditure gradually declined from 41.4 per cent in 1991-92 to 37.0 per cent in 1996-97 and rose again slightly to 37.2 per cent in 1997-98 (RE) and again to 37.9 per cent in 1998-99 (B.E).

27.4.1 One of the important reasons for continued massive increase in revenue expenditure is the increasing interest liability of the Central Government on its debt and other liabilities. Apart from more funds borrowed for capital expenditure, increase in borrowings was also for meeting revenue deficits, thus adding to the interest liability as mentioned earlier in paragraph 25.1.1. As a result interest on such borrowed funds utilised for meeting revenue deficit has increased further the revenue expenditure resulting in higher revenue deficits, for meeting which more borrowed funds became necessary. Thus a vicious circle has been created in which revenue deficit chases borrowed funds, the interest on which creates more revenue deficit needing more borrowed funds without any halt. The growth in expenditure on interest during the period from 1970-71 to 1990-91 is indicated below:

Year	Total Revenue expenditure (Rs. crore)	Expenditure on interest payment (Rs. crore)	Rate of growth of interest payment (in per cent)	Expenditure on interest as per cent of total revenue expenditure
1	2*	3*	4	5
1970-71	3179	606	–	19

(Contd.)

1	2*	3*	4	5
1975-76	7189	1228	–	17
1976-77	8441	1488	21	18
1977-78	9362	1646	11	18
1978-79	10948	1984	21	18
1979-80	12034	2292	16	19
1980-81	14544	2748	20	19
1981-82	15868	3260	19	21
1982-83	19346	4007	23	21
1983-84	22890	4869	22	21
1984-85	27881	6050	24	22
1985-86	34722	7504	24	22
1986-87	42544	9237	23	22
1987-88	48129	11236	22	23
1988-89	56255	14261	27	25
1989-90	66528	17735	24	27
1990-91	76212	21471	21	28

* *Source* : Reports on Currency and Finance of the Reserve Bank of India.

27.4.2 Although there was variation in the rate of growth of expenditure on interest payment between 11 per cent and 27 per cent during the period from 1976-77 to 1990-91, the share of interest payments to total revenue expenditure remained at 18 per cent in 1976-77, 1977-78 and 1978-79, increased to 19 per cent in 1979-80 and 1980-81, increased further and remained at 21 per cent in the years 1981-82, 1982-83 and 1983-84.

In the years 1984-85 to 1986-87, the share of expenditure on interest payments remained at 22 per cent of the total revenue expenditure and increased further to 23 per cent in 1987-88 and 25 per cent in the year 1988-89. The expenditure on interest payments increased to 27 per cent of the total revenue expenditure in 1989-90. In 1990-91, the expenditure on interest payment increased to 28 per cent of the total revenue expenditure.

27.4.3 The growth in expenditure on interest payment during the period from 1991-92 onwards is indicated below:

Year	Total revenue expenditure (Rs. crores)	Expenditure on interest payment (Rs. crores)	Rate of growth of interest payment (in percent)	Expenditure on interest as per cent of total revenue expenditure
1	2	3	4	5
1991-92	85,361	26,596	24	31
1992-93	96,147	31,075	17	32
1993-94	1,12,366	36,740	18	33
1994-95	1,26,578	44,060	20	35
1995-96	1,44,644	50,045	14	35
1996-97	1,64,340	59,478	19	36
1997-98 (RE)	1,89,459	65,700	15	35
1998-99 (BE)	2,18,368	75,000	14	34

Source : Reports on Currency and Finance of the Reserve Bank of India.

27.4.4 The above table shows that the rate of growth of interest payment varied between 14 per cent and 24 per cent during the period from 1991-92 to 1998-99 (B.E.); the rate has remained below 20 per cent except in 1991-92 (24 per cent) and 1994-95 (20 per cent).

Expenditure on interest payment varied between 31 per cent and 36 per cent of total revenue expenditure during the period from 1991-92 to 1998-99 (B.E.). The share of interest payment in total revenue expenditure was substantially more than that in the pre-financial reforms period upto 1990-91.

27.4.5 It is true that the Central Government earns interest by re-lending the borrowed funds in the main, partly to State Government and also substantially to public sector undertakings. But due to massive increase in interest payment liability, the net interest payment liability has been on the increase substantially. The benefits derived from the borrowed funds invested in development projects directly by Government are not in the shape of interest or dividend. For example, the benefits directly derived from an irrigation project by the Government may be in the form of irrigation charges collected from the beneficiaries, but as a result of irrigation the agricultural production increases giving a boost to the economy for the country, which in turn ultimately improves the budgetary position of Government. As mentioned earlier in paragraph 23, the returns from such investments of borrowed funds have not been satisfactory necessitating more borrowed funds for developmental purposes. In addition, as mentioned in paragraph 27.4.1, since 1979-80 borrowed funds are being utilised for meeting revenue deficits i.e. the portion of revenue expenditure which is in excess of revenue receipts. As described by Shri D.H. Panandikar (Paragraph 27.1.3) when money is spent on revenue expenditure (consumption expenditure) it vanishes. In other words, borrowed funds which are not only expected to remain intact in the shape of durable assets to generate income or liquidate future liability (when utilised for liquidating future liability) are being utilised since 1979-80 on revenue (consumption) expenditure when the money just vanishes leaving behind not only liability in capital account for repayment of borrowed funds by further borrowings but also the liability on revenue account for repayment of interest.

27.4.6 The other item of expenditure which has inflated the revenue expenditure is the payment of subsidy. The following table shows how the expenditure on subsidy has increased during the period from 1975-76 to 1990-91:

Year	Total revenue expenditure (Rs. crores)	Expenditure on payment of subsidy (Rs. crores)	Rate of growth of payment of subsidy	Expenditure on subsidy as per cent of total revenue expenditure
1	2	3	4	5
1975-76	7189	470	–	7
1976-77	8441	974	107	12
1977-78	9362	1287	31	14
1978-79	10948	1504(RE)	17	14
1979-80	12034	1831(RE)	22	15
1980-81	14544	2028	4	13
1981-82	15868	1941	-4	12
1982-83	19346	2262	17	12
1983-84	22890	2749	22	12
1984-85	27881	4038	47	14

(Contd.)

1	2	3	4	5
1985-86	34722	4796	19	14
1986-87	42544	5451	14	13
1987-88	48129	5980	10	12
1988-89	56255	7732	29	14
1989-90	66528	10677	38	16
1990-91	76212	12121	14	16

Source : (a) Column 2 : Reports on Currency and Finance of Reserve Bank of India.
(b) Column 3 : (i) 1983-84 onwards from the Expenditure Budget, Volume 1, 1991-92.
(ii) For others years, the figures have been taken from Economic Surveys, Reports on Currency & Finance and Budget documents.

27.4.7 It will appear from the above table that the expenditure on subsidy, which was merely 7 per cent of the total revenue expenditure in 1975-76, increased to 12 per cent of that in 1976-77 and further increased to 14 per cent in 1977-78. Thus in a span of three years ending 1977-78 the share of expenditure on subsidy to the total revenue expenditure increased by 100 per cent. In 1978-79 and 1979-80 the share of expenditure on subsidy to total revenue expenditure was 14 and 15 per cent respectively. In the Economic Survey for 1980-81, the need for curtailing budgetary subsidies was emphasised. Thus we find that expenditure on subsidy in 1981-82 decreased by Rs. 87 crores as compared to 1980-81. During the years 1980-81 to 1983-84, the share of expenditure on subsidy to the total revenue expenditure remained between 12 and 13 per cent. However, this increased to 14 per cent in 1984-85 and remained so in 1985-86 and then declined to 13 per cent in 1986-87 and 12 per cent in 1987-88. In 1988-89, the share of expenditure on subsidy to the total revenue expenditure was 14 per cent, which was expected to rise to 16 per cent according to the revised estimate for 1989-90 and remain so in the budget estimate for 1990-91.

27.4.8 The expenditure on subsidy increased by 364 per cent in a decade from Rs. 1287 crores in 1977-78 to Rs. 5980 crores in 1987-88. In 1988-89 (Rs. 7732 crores), the expenditure on subsidy was 500 per cent more than the actual expenditure in 1977-78, while in 1989-90 (Rs. 10677 crores) the same was 730 per cent more than the actual expenditure of

1977-78. The following table gives the breakup of the total expenditure on subsidy for certain years on different items of subsidy.

Year	Food	Fertilisers	Export promotion	Other subsidies	Total
		(Rupees in Crores)			
1976-77	506	60	269	139	974
1977-78	480	266	327	214	1287
1980-81	650	505	399	474	2028
1981-82	700	381	477	383	1941
1982-83	711	603	477	471	2262
1983-84	835	1042	463	409	2749
1984-85	1101	1928	518	491	4038
1985-86	1650	1924	603	619	4796
1986-87	2000	1898	785	768	5451
1987-88	2000	2164	962	854	5980
1988-89	2200	3201	1386	945	7732
1989-90	2476	4601	2089	1511	10677
1990-91	2450	4389	2742	2577	12158

Sources : 1. Expenditure Budget, Volume I, for 1991-92 for the years 1983-84 onwards.
2. Figures for earlier years have been taken from Reports on Currency and Finance, Economic Surveys and Budget documents.

The subsidy on food which amounted to Rs. 480 crores in 1977-78 reached the level Rs. 2000 crores (an increase of 317 per cent) in a decade ending 1987-88. The subsidy on food increased to Rs. 2200 crores in 1988-89 and Rs. 2476 crores in 1989-90. The subsidy on fertilizers increased from Rs. 266 crores in 1977-78 by 714 per cent to Rs. 2164 crores in a decade ending 1987-88. As compared to 1987-88, the subsidy on fertilizer was estimated to further rise by 48 per cent in 1988-89 (Rs. 3201 crores) and by 113 per cent to Rs. 4601 crores in a 1989-90. Subsidy on export promotion increased in a decade by 193 per cent from Rs. 327 crores in 1977-78 to Rs. 962 crores in 1987-88, and increased by about 44 per cent more in 1988-89 (Rs. 1386 crores) compared to 1987-88. In 1989-90, the export promotion subsidy rose further to Rs. 2089 crores (an increase of about 51 per cent as compared to 1988-89).

27.4.9 In the post-financial reforms period, i.e., since 1991-92, the increase in expenditure on subsidy is indicated below:

Year	Total revenue expenditure (Rs. crores)	Expenditure on subsidy (Rs. crores)	Rate of growth of payment of subsidy (per cent)	Expenditure on subsidy as per cent of total revenue expenditure
1991-92	85,361.00	12,253	1	14
1992-93	96,147.00	11,995	-2	12
1993-94	1,12,366.00	12,682	6	11
1994-95	1,26,578.00	12,932	2	10
1995-96	1,44,644.00	13,372	3	9
1996-97	1,64,340.00	16,364	22	10
1997-98(RE)	1,89,459.00	19,487	19	10
1998-99(BE)	2,18,368.00	24,683	27	11

Source : The figures of subsidy have been taken from the Expenditure Budget, Vol I, 1999-2000.

27.4.10 It is noticed from the above table that in the post-financial reforms period, the share of expenditure on subsidy in total revenue expenditure has declined to some extent. However, as compared to the total expenditure on subsidy in 1990-91 (Rs. 12121.0 crores) the same in 1998-99 (B.E) is more than double. The rate of growth of expenditure on subsidy since 1996-97 has increased considerably. Just after the financial reforms were started, the rate of growth of expenditure on subsidy was comparatively much less in 1991-92 (1 per cent), 1992-93 (-2 per cent), 1993-94 (6 per cent), 1994-95 (2 per cent), 1995-96 (3 per cent). This shot up to 22 per cent in 1996-97, came down slightly to 19 per cent in 1997-98 (R.E.), but again went up to 27 per cent in 1997-98 (B.E.).

27.4.11 The following table gives the itemwise total expenditure on subsidy for the period 1991-92 to 1998-99 (B.E.):

Year	Food	Fertiliser	Export promotion	Other subsidy	Total
(Rs. in Crores)					
1	2	3	4	5	6
1991-92	2850	5185	1758	2460	12,253
1992-93	2800	5796	818	2581	11,995
1993-94	5537	4562	665	1918	12,682

(Contd.)

1	2	3	4	5	6
1994-95	5100	5769	658	1405	12,932
1995-96	5377	6735	318	942	13,372
1996-97	6066	7578	397	2320	16,364
1997-98	7500	9918	420	1649	19,487
1998-99(RE)	8700	11388	575	4020	24,683

Source : The figures have been taken from the Expenditure Budget, Vol I, 1999-2000.

The subsidy on Food in 1998-99, RE, (Rs. 8700.0 crores) is 255 per cent more than that in 1990-91 (Rs. 2450.0 crores). Similarly, the subsidy on fertilizers in 1998-99, RE (Rs. 11,388.0 crores) is 160 per cent more than that in 1990-91 (Rs. 4389.0 crores). Other subsidies increased by 56 per cent in 1998-99, RE, (Rs. 4020.0 crores) as compared to that in 1990-91 (Rs. 2577.0 crores).

27.4.12 It may be mentioned in this connection that according to the budget for 1999-2000, the total expenditure on subsidy is estimated as Rs. 23838.0 crores, which is a little less than that in 1998-99, R.E., (Rs. 24683.0 crores). The subsidy on food in 1999-2000 is estimated as Rs. 8700.0 crores, which is Rs. 500.0 crores less than 1998-99, R.E., (Rs. 8700.0 crores). The subsidy on fertilizers is estimated as Rs. 13,250.0 crores in 1999-2000 against Rs. 11,388.0 crores in 1998-99 (R.E). The subsidy on export promotion in 1999-2000 is estimated as Rs. 630.0 crores, which is a little higher than Rs. 575.0 crores in 1998-99 (R.E.). The expenditure on other subsidies in 1999-2000 is estimated as Rs. 1758.0 crores which is substantially less than that in 1998-99 (RE).

It may be pointed out here that apart from such overt items of subsidy which appear in budget documents and accounts, there are covert subsidies which have not been quantified. For example, electricity or irrigation water supplied free or at concessional prices by the States. Such hidden subsidies provided by States affect their finances, resulting in more transfers from Centre. The Central Government also provides such hidden subsidy, for example, subsidised price charged from consumers of L.P.G. If all such hidden subsidies are quantified, it will be found that the liability of the nation on subsidy is much more than that what appears in the budget and accounts. In planning restoration of financial health of the nation, such quantification has become very necessary, for elimination, at least gradually.

27.5.1 Thus it will appear that expenditure on interest and subsidy accounted for 35 per cent of the total revenue expenditure in 1987-88. Their share in total revenue expenditure rose to 39 per cent in 1988-89 and to 42 per cent in 1989-90. The total share of interest and subsidy in total revenue expenditure increased further to 45 per cent both in 1997-98 (R.E.) and 1998-99 (B.E.). Unless, therefore, economy is effected in expenditure on payment of interest and subsidy, which together account for about 45 per cent of the total revenue expenditure, it will be impossible to avoid revenue deficit.

27.5.2 Reduction in expenditure on interest and subsidy is all the more important, as the other major elements of revenue expenditure in the shape of pay and allowances of Government servants and pension to retired employees have been continuing to rise, consequent on release of half-yearly instalments of dearness allowance with reference to the ever rising cost of living index. In this context, the question of restricting the number of Central Government employees, which had been rising as follows, needs serious consideration.

Year	Number of Central Govt. employees (in lakhs)
1971	28.36
1976	30.74
1981	31.95
1984	33.33
1985	33.40
1986	33.41
1987	33.50
1988	33.87
1989	33.95
1990	33.97
1991	34.10
1992	34.28
1993	33.83
1994	33.92
1995	38.95
1996	33.66
1997	32.95

It appears that there was an attempt to restrict the increase in the number of Central Government employees.

27.5.3 Some of the relevant observations about revenue expenditure in the speeches of the Finance Ministers, in the Economic Surveys and also in the Reports on Currency and Finance are quoted hereafter:

(a) In this connection it may be pointed out that the Economic Survey for 1990-91 observed in paragraph 7.7 that "The immediate task is to check the fiscal imbalances before the situation assumes alarming proportion. As a first step, the emphasis should be on curtailing unproductive expenditure and ensuring a fair minimum return from the investments made in the public sector undertakings."

Despite above stipulation revenue expenditure increased from Rs. 83,630 crores in the revised estimate of 1991-92 to Rs. 89,570 crores according to the budget for 1992-93. The expenditure on interest payments and subsidy in both these years was estimated to exceed 47 per cent of revenue expenditure.

(b) The Economic Survey for 1991-92 (Part II - paragraph 2.4) has observed as follows:

Such a fiscal situation has become unsustainable. Interest payments on accumulated debts constitute about 24 per cent of total expenditure of the Central Government. Unless firmly dealt with by checking expenditure and raising revenues, such a situation would result in the absorption of an increasing proportion of Government resources necessitating higher borrowings simply to service the past debts, thus pushing the Government into a debt trap. The unabated growth of Government expenditure, particularly non-plan expenditure, has been the main reason for the country falling into the present fiscal crisis. A comparison of the Seventh Plan projections of selected fiscal indicators as annualised in the Long Term Fiscal Policy (LTFP) document with the actuals, reveals that throughout the Seventh Plan period, the balance from current revenue (BCR) remained negative and even deteriorated to (-) 1.2 per cent of GDP in 1980-90, the terminal year of Seventh Plan, as compared with the projection of positive BCR of

0.2 per cent of GDP. The comparison also reveals that the performance of direct taxes has been lower than the targets. In financing the Seventh Plan, the shares of domestic borrowings and budgetary deficit far exceeded the targets. Causatively, non-plan revenue expenditure, particularly, on defence, interest payments and food and fertilizer subsidies rose sharply and exceeded the targets. The process of fiscal adjustment cannot be postponed any further. In the present scenario, there are no soft options and no time to lose."

[*Note*: BCR is the balance of current receipts (excluding external grants) over non-plan revenue expenditure.]

(c) In the Economic Survey for 1991-92, the need for reducing subsidy was emphasised in the fiscal policy enunciated as follows:

"The immediate aim of fiscal policy must be to improve the fiscal balance in order to estimate the inflationary pressure emanating from the budget deficit. The other objectives of fiscal policy reform would be to stop further accumulation of public debt to reduce the level of subsidies in the economy and eliminate open-ended cross-subsidization, to direct Government expenditure towards providing essential public services of high quality; and finally to restore Government's capacity to make strategic investments in infrastructure and human resources, guide the economy and look after the weak and privileged."

(d) In the above context the following observations in the speech of the Finance Minister in presenting the budget of 1992-93 are relevant:

"The Eighth Five Year Plan commences from 1 April 1992 and aims at the objective of achieving near full employment in a period of ten years. The investment requirements of every sector are large, and it is important that plan allocations should enable implementing to make a good start, especially in the infrastructure sectors. However, we have had to work within the limits imposed by the continuing need to restore macro-economic balance, which is essential if we are to contain inflation and manage the balance of payments. This calls for a further reduction in the fiscal deficit in 1992-93. Larger Plan expenditure can be accommodated within a smaller fiscal deficit if, apart from increasing tax and non-tax revenues, Government, non-Plan expenditure can be contained. I must admit that this has been a daunting task."

The total non-Plan expenditure in the budget for 1992-93 was shown as Rs. 84,475 crores as against Rs. 80,070 crores in the revised estimate for 1991-92.

The Finance Minister also made the following observations in his speech while presenting the budget for 1992-93:

"Interest charges are the largest single item for non-Plan expenditure........... This item can be controlled only by reducing the reliance on borrowed funds; and I intend to do this by reducing the fiscal deficit for 1992-93. However, the benefit of this action will be felt only by Finance Ministers presenting the budget in future............".

"Subsidies are another important component in non-Plan expenditure. Last year, Food, Fertilizer and Export subsidies were the three major subsidies and their rapid growth has been one of the main factors behind the unchecked growth of non-Plan expenditure. We made an important change this year by abolishing export subsidies. However, some subsidy payments still remain in the pipeline, and I am providing Rs. 480 crores on this account."

"Food subsidy is a part of our system of food security for the poorer and weaker sections of our population and is a basic element in our social policy .... The allocation for these items will be augmented in the course of the year to meet the requirements fully."

"This brings me to fertiliser subsidy which has grown into the largest single subsidy in our system. There is no doubt that fertiliser is an essential ingredient for agricultural production, and agricultural development is vital not only for economic growth in general, but also to ensure rising levels of income and employment in rural areas. In 1980-81, the fertiliser subsidy was 12% of the total allocation in the Central and State Plans taken together for Agriculture, Rural Development, Special Area Programmes and Irrigation and Flood Control. It increased to 33% in 1991-92. A Parliamentary Committee is currently looking into the whole issue of fertiliser pricing and subsidy including alternatives for restructuring the subsidy. I propose to wait for the report of this committee and take a view on this matter later in the year.........."

"Other items of non-Plan expenditure have been tightly constrained in the allocations provided to keep the fiscal deficit within manageable levels............"

(e) The Economic Survey for 1992-93 observed as follows (paragraph 2.8):

"The steady growth of Government expenditure, particularly non-plan expenditure, has been main reason for the country falling into a fiscal crisis. A significant element of this is the growth in interest payments, which in an efficient system would have been fully covered by returns on productive capital expenditure and investment financed by debt. Instead of providing such a cover, plan expenditure has been characterized by low returns from investments and inefficiency. This has resulted in wastage of scarce resources. The decreasing share of plan expenditure going for capital expenditure has further compounded the problem. Seventh Plan projections of selected fiscal indicators (interpolated for the 2nd to the 4th year of the Plan in the long-term fiscal policy), envisaged a positive balance of current revenue (BCR) of the Centre of 0.2 per cent of GDP by 1989-90. A comparison with actual performance reveals that throughout the Seventh Plan period, the BCR remained negative and even deteriorated to -1.2 per cent of GDP in 1989-90, the terminal year of the Seventh Plan. One reason was that direct tax collections were lower than targeted. On the financing side the share of domestic borrowings and the budgetary deficit far exceeded the targets. Interest payments, food and fertilizers subsidy also rose sharply and also exceeded the targets".

(f) It was stated in the Economic Survey for 1993-94 (paragraph 14) that, "The growth in internal and external liabilities and the increasing rate of interest have resulted in a mounting burden of interest payments. While gross interest payments as a ratio of total expenditure almost doubled from 11.6 per cent in 1980-81 to 20.5 per cent in 1990-91, interest payments net of interest received increased by three times from 3.6 per cent to 12.1 per cent. Between 1990-91 and 1992-93 (RE) interest payments on internal liabilities increased by Rs. 9241 crores. Based on the stock of debt at the end of 1989-90 and the interest rate prevailing in 1990-91, it is seen that about 25 per cent of this rise in interest payment is due to the rise in the average interest rate. The remaining 75 per cent is due to the increase in debt during 1990-91 and 1991-92. The rise in debt is equal to the fiscal deficit which itself contains interest payments on past debt. More than half of the increase in debt can, therefore, be attributed to interest payments during 1990-91 and 1991-92 on the debt which existed at the end of 1989-90. The increase in debt attributable to the primary fiscal deficit, contributed only 33 per cent of the increase in interest payments".

(g) In introducing the budget for 1994-95, the then Finance Minister, Shri Manmohan Singh had observed as follows (paragraph 49):

"I have to draw the attention of the Honourable Members to a major factor which has been contributing to the sizeable increase in non-plan expenditure year after year, and this is the interest burden. The provision for interest payments next year is placed at Rs. 46,000 crores. This is an increase of Rs. 8,000 crores over the current year's Budget estimates whereas the increase in total non-plan expenditure is Rs. 15,045 crores. Honourable Members will appreciate that the major part of the interest burden is a legacy from the past and it continues to grow because of the continued high level of Government borrowing. Interest payments can be reduced only if we can implement a programme of phased reduction in the Government's total borrowing requirements or fiscal deficit. This can become a reality only if our tax system becomes more buoyant, our public enterprises generate more internal resources and we reduce expenditure on subsidies. A bold programme for disinvestment of government equity in public enterprises and earmarking a part of the sale proceeds purely for debt reduction would also be of great help".

(h) In introducing the interim budget for 1996-97, the Finance Minister, Shri Manmohan Singh observed (paragraph 35) as follows:

"A major factor which has been contributing to the sizeable increase in our non-Plan expenditure is the interest burden. The provision for interest payments during 1996-97 is estimated to be Rs. 60,000 crores as against Rs. 52,000 crores in the current year. Interest payments represent mainly the legacy of past borrowings. Indeed, they would have been even higher but for our success in reducing the fiscal deficit in recent years. Members will appreciate that our emphasis on reducing the fiscal deficit will pay rich dividends in the form of reduction of interest burden in the years to come. There should be no slackening in our resolve to bring the fiscal deficit to a more manageable and affordable level. This together with continued reforms of our tax system, generation of more internal resources by public sector enterprises, greater disinvestment in public sector enterprises and containing subsidies to affordable levels will free resources for higher priority development needs".

(i) In his speech, the then Finance Minister, Shri P. Chidambaram had said (paragraph 28) while presenting the final budget for 1996-97 that, "The budget challenge that we face is the fiscal challenge. The United Front government is committed to bringing the fiscal deficit to below 4% of GDP. This is what the Common Minimum Programme says and this is what I intend to do over a period of time. One plank of the strategy is, of course, to raise more revenues. But without a credible public expenditure management policy, no programme of fiscal deficit reduction will be sustained. I believe that no one is against austerity or efficiency as such. At the same time, I accept the position that sound expenditure management is not a mere technocratic exercise but involves issues of equity, fairness and non-discrimination. In order to work out a reasonable policy in this regard, I propose to appoint a high-level Expenditure Management and Reforms Commission comprising distinguished political leaders, economists and administrators. This Commission will be given four months–and I hope no more–to submit its recommendations on public expenditure management and control as far as the Central Government is concerned. The report will be made public immediately so that we can generate an informed public debate on an issue that has a vital bearing on our economic future".

(j) The Economic Survey for 1996-97 stated as follows (paragraph 30):

"The reduction in the fiscal deficit has been attempted through an increase in revenues coupled with a reduction in expenditure. Revenue receipts (net) are budgeted to increase by 18.3 per cent during 1996-97. These receipts, as a proportion of GDP, are to edge up from 10 per cent in 1995-96 (RE) to 10.4 per cent in 1996-97 (BE). Despite a larger outgo on account of interest payments (Rs. 60,000 crores), subsidies (Rs. 16,320 crores) and provision for revision of salaries and pension benefits (Rs. 4,000 crores), total revenue expenditure is budgeted to grow at a lower rate to 12.7 per cent compared with 17.5 per cent in 1995-96 (RE). This deceleration in the growth of revenue expenditure has led to a decline in the revenue expenditure to GDP ratio from 13.1 per cent in 1995-96 (RE) to 12.9 per cent in 1996-97 (BE). This favourable outcome on the expenditure side is largely on account of containment of non-interest non-plan expenditure growth at 9.3 per cent during 1996-97 (BE), about half the growth of 18.8 per cent in 1995-96 (RE). Consequently, non-interest revenue expenditure as a proportion of GDP is budgeted to fall to 8.1 per cent from 8.3 per cent in 1995-96 (RE). The revenue deficit is budgeted to fall by 0.5 per cent point of GDP."

(k) While presenting the budget for 1997-98, the then Finance Minister, Shri P. Chidambaram had said (paragraph 6) as follows:

"The one commitment that I have not been able to keep is to set up Expenditure Management and Reforms Commission. I failed because I wanted an 'A' team and I was not content with a 'B' team. Key members of the 'A' team are in this House and in the Rajya Sabha, and they still elude me. I shall keep trying. Meanwhile, I have not let up on my resolve to keep expenditure within the Budget and I have achieved a fair measure of success."

(1) In presenting the budget for 1999-2000, the then Finance Minister, Shri Yashwant Sinha said as follows (paragraph 30):

"The high rate of growth of non-developmental expenditure by Government is a growing and critical source of concern. I propose the following initiatives:

* The most effective and lasting solution to this problem is to begin the process of downsizing Government. We are making an immediate beginning by abolishing four Secretary-level posts through a process of merger and rationalisation of Central Government departments. This will take effect on April 1, 1999.
* To carry this process forward in a systematic way towards reducing the role and the administrative structure of the Government, we will constitute an Expenditure Reforms Commission headed by an eminent and experienced person.
* In preparation for the next Budget, I propose to initiate a system of Zero Base Budgeting.
* To promote transparency and curb the growth of contingent government liabilities, Government has decided to establish a Guarantee Redemption Fund with an initial corpus of Rs. 50 crores. I encourage all State Governments to set up similar Funds.

27.5.4 It will appear from the above that there is no dearth of platitudes, pedantry and promises for control over expenditure, which had no effect on growth of revenue expenditure.

III

EXPENDITURE ON CAPITAL ACCOUNT

28.1.1 As has already been mentioned earlier, capital expenditure is incurred usually from borrowed funds with the object of either increasing durable assets or reducing recurring liabilities. The expression borrowed funds also include the net funds available in the Public Account. As has been mentioned in paragraph 3.4.3 of my book "*Fundamentals of Government Budgeting in India*", it is only logical to meet capital expenditure from borrowed funds, the liabilities in respect of which are spread over a number of years, as the benefits arising from capital expenditure flow over a period of several years. In principle, however, capital expenditure may also be met from revenues, provided there is a revenue surplus. But in reality, since 1979-80 there has been a revenue deficit in each year end, as such, the question of meeting capital expenditure from revenues did not arise.

It may be mentioned in this connection that capital receipts, so far as they relate to the expenditure during the implementation of a project and accruing during that period, are utilised in reduction of capital expenditure.

28.1.2 The following table indicates the growth of capital expenditure, as compared to capital receipts, over the years, upto 1990-91, i.e. before the financial reforms were started:

Year	Total capital receipts (Rs. crores)	Rate of growth of Capital Receipts (in per cent)	Total capital expenditure (Rs. crores)	Rate of growth of Capital Expenditure (in per cent)
1	2*	3	4*	5
1950-51	105	–	183	–

(Contd.)

1	2*	3	4*	5
1960-61 (as compared to 1950-51)	1127	984	1001	447
1970-71 (as compared to 1960-61)	2524	124	2972	197
1975-76 as compared to1970-71)	4697	86	5950	100
1976-77	5573	19	6016	1
1977-78	5588	0.4	6951	16
1978-79	6938	24	8736	26
1979-80	6125	-12	7864	-10
1980-81	9432	54	10295	31
1981-82	10156	8	11254	9
1982-83	12483	23	12884	14
1983-84	15861	27	14881	16
1984-85	17768	12	18016	21
1985-86	16708	-6	16135	-10
1986-87	18259	11	19014	18
1987-88	22026	19	18705	-2
1988-89	25673	17	20800	10
1989-90	30,020	17	28698	38
1990-91	38,997	30	31782	17

* *Source* : Reports on Currency and Finance of the Reserve Bank of India.

From the above table no uniformity emerges in the growth of either the capital receipts or the capital expenditure, despite the planned development which the country has been attempting since 1951-52. If the actuals shown in the above table are taken into account, the highest capital expenditure of Rs. 20800 crores was incurred in 1988-89; this expenditure was 11266 per cent more than that in 1950-51 (Rs. 183 crores) i.e. the year preceding the year (1951-52) in which planning started. In the same period, the capital receipts increased by 24350 per cent in 1988-89 (Rs. 25673 crores) as compared to that in 1950-51 (Rs. 105 crores). In 1987-88, although the capital receipts increased by 19 per cent to Rs. 22026 crores, as compared to 1986-87 (Rs. 18529 crores), the expenditure declined by 2 per cent to Rs. 18705 crores as compared to 1986-87 (Rs. 19014 crores). In 1988-89, the capital expenditure of Rs. 20800 crores was 10 per cent more than that of 1987-88 (Rs. 18705 crores). The increase of capital receipt was, however, 17 per cent in 1988-89 compared to that of 1987-88. The revised estimate for 1989-90 (Rs. 23692 crores) showed a decline in capital receipts by 8 per cent as compared to 1988-89, while the capital expenditure showed an increase of 11 per cent to Rs. 23006 crores. The budget estimate for 1990-91 indicated an increase of 24 per cent in capital receipts, while the increase in capital expenditure was estimated at a moderate 2 per cent.

In the years 1979-80 and 1985-86, there was deceleration of both capital receipts and capital expenditure. While in 1979-80 the capital receipts (Rs. 6125 crores) declined by 12 per cent as compared to the preceding year (Rs. 6938 crores), the capital expenditure (Rs. 7864 crores) declined by 10 per cent as compared to 1978-79 (Rs. 8736 crores). In other words, the rate of decline of capital expenditure was less than that of capital receipts. The position was, however, reverse in 1985-86 when the rate of decline of capital receipts was less than that of capital expenditure. In 1985-86, the capital receipts (Rs. 16708 crores) declined by 6 per cent as compared to that of 1984-85 (Rs. 17,768 crores). On the other hand, capital expenditure declined by 10 per cent from Rs. 18016 crores in 1984-85 to Rs. 16135 crores in 1985-86.

28.1.3 The following table shows the growth of capital expenditure as compared to capital receipts from 1991-92 to 1998-99 (B.E.):

Year	Total Capital receipts	Rate of growth of Capital receipts	Total Capital expenditure	Rate of growth of Capital expenditure
1	2	3	4	5
1991-92	38,528	(-)1	29,122	(-)8
1992-93	36,178	(-)6	29,916	3
1993-94	55,440	35	33,684	13

(Contd.)

1	2	3	4	5
1994-95	68,695	24	38,627	13
1995-96	58,338	(-)15	38,415	(-)1
1996-97	61,544	5	42,074	10
1997-98 (RE)	96,731	57	53,045	25
1998-99 (BE)	1,05,933	10	57,865	9

During the period from 1991-92 to 1998-99 (B.E.) also no uniformity emerges either in the growth of capital receipts or in the growth of capital expenditure. During this period the capital receipts increased enormously from Rs. 38,528.0 crores in 1991-92 to Rs. 1,05,933 crores in 1998-99 (B.E.); the increase was about 178 per cent. There was increase in capital expenditure also from Rs. 29,122.0 crores in 1991-92 to Rs. 57,865.0 crores in 1998-99 (B.E); the increase was almost 100 per cent. Capital receipts declined to some extent in 1991-92, 1992-93 and 1995-96. Capital expenditure declined to some extent in 1991-92 and 1995-96. In all the above years, capital expenditure was less then capital receipts indicating that capital receipts were utilised for revenue expenditure.

PART IV – SURPLUS/DEFICIT

Chapters

I

REVENUE SURPLUS/DEFICIT

29.1.1 When the revenue receipts exceed the revenue expenditure, the difference is revenue surplus. If, however, the revenue receipts fall short of the expenditure, the difference is revenue deficit.

As mentioned earlier in paragraph 26.1.1, the most prudent financial policy is that revenue receipts should not only meet in full the revenue expenditure, which is actually consumption expenditure (according to the words of Sh. Panandikar quoted in paragraph 26.1.3 money spent on consumption i.e. revenue expenditure just vanishes), but also be sufficient to generate a surplus for financing capital expenditure. As will be evident from the following table, the sound financial policy mentioned above was followed by the Central Government till 1978-79.

(Rs. in Crores)

Year	Total Revenue Receipts	Total Revenue Expenditure	Surplus	Deficit
1	2	3	4	5
1950-51	406	347	59	–
1960-61	877	826	51	–
1970-71	3342	3179	163	–
1974-75	6557	5793	764	–
1975-76	8075	7188	887	–
1976-77	8753	8441	312	–
1977-78	9792	9362	430	–
1978-79	11240	10948	292	–
1979-80	11340	12034		694
1980-81	12829	14544		1715
1981-82	15574	15868		294
1982-83	18091	19346		1255

(Contd.)

1	2	3	4	5
1983-84	20493	22890		2397
1984-85	24384	27881		3497
1985-86	28884	34772		5888
1986-87	34768	42544		7776
1987-88	38992	48129		9137
1988-89	45740	56255		10515
1989-90	54614	66528		11914
1990-91	57650	76212		18567

29.1.2 The above Table shows that revenue surplus (Rs. 59 crores) was 12 per cent of the total revenue receipts (Rs. 406 crores) in 1950-51. In 1960-61, revenue surplus (Rs. 51 crores) had declined to 6 per cent of the total revenue receipts (Rs. 877 crores). This further declined to 5 per cent in 1970-71 when the revenue surplus was Rs. 163 crores as compared to the total revenue receipts amounting to Rs. 3342 crores. As mentioned in paragraph 26.1.5 certain anti-inflationary measures were taken in July 1974, of which two measures were directly for improving the budgetary position of the Central Government. These measures and other economy measures taken by the Central Government resulted in a higher revenue surplus (Rs. 764 crores) in 1974-75 which was more than 11 per cent of the total revenue receipts in that year (Rs. 6557 crores). The subsequent year (1975-76) had a larger surplus (Rs. 887 crores) which was 12 per cent of the total revenue receipts (Rs. 8075 crores).

Thereafter, the revenue surplus declined to Rs. 312 crores (about 4 per cent of the total revenue receipts of Rs. 8753 crores) in 1976-77. In 1977-78, the revenue surplus (Rs. 430 crores) was a little more than 4 per cent of the total revenue receipts (Rs. 9792 crores). The revenue surplus declined again to Rs. 292 crores in 1978-79, which was less than 3 per cent of the total revenue receipts of Rs. 11240 crores.

29.1.3 The year 1979-80 was a turning point in budgetary history of the country when for the first time the Central Government had a revenue deficit of Rs. 694 crores which was almost 6 per cent of the total revenue expenditure of Rs. 12034 crores. In the Economic Survey for 1986-87, this was attempted to be explained as follows:

"The Centre's revenue account, which used to be in surplus, turned into deficit in 1979-80 following a larger devolution of resources by the Seventh Finance Commission, particularly doubling of the States' share in Union Excise Duties from 20 per cent to 40 per cent ..."

The fact, however, remains that the revenue expenditure had also been rising at an alarming pace as shown in the preceding paragraph.

The revenue deficit has since then (1979-80) been continuing.

29.1.4 In 1980-81, the revenue deficit increased to Rs. 1715 crores which was almost 12 per cent of the total expenditure of Rs. 14544 crores. The Economic Survey for 1980-81 claimed that "from the middle of the fiscal year 1980-81 the economy was able to recover most of the ground lost during 1979-80." But the year ended with a larger revenue deficit as compared to 1979-80. As for the reasons for the same, the Economic Survey for 1980-81 mentioned *inter alia* that there was additional expenditure on relief assistance to States on account of drought, generation of resources within the public sector was lower than anticipated because of continuing production difficulties and rising costs and there was additional expenditure on increasing interest burden.

29.1.5 The revenue deficit decreased to Rs. 294 crores in 1981-82, which was less than 2 per cent of the total revenue expenditure of that year (Rs. 15868 crores). The Economic Survey for 1981-82 stated that "the Central Government made massive efforts to mobilise additional resources in 1981-82".

29.1.6 In 1982-83, again the revenue deficit increased to Rs. 1255 crores, which was in excess of 6 per cent of the total revenue expenditure of Rs. 19346 crores. The Economic Survey for 1982-83 stated that "the growth in tax receipts has so far been significantly lower than anticipated in the budget. On the other hand, there have been substantial increases in expenditure on account of drought and other natural calamities relief......". The Economic Survey for 1983-84 also observed that in 1982-83 "the budgetary position of the

Central Government was marked by relatively slow growth of tax revenues and a sharp increase in non-developmental expenditure".

29.1.7 The revenue deficit increased to Rs. 2397 crores in 1983-84 which was more than 10 per cent of the total revenue expenditure of Rs. 22890 crores. The Economic Survey for 1983-84 pointed out that there "was a build up of pressure on the Central Budget in the course of the year. Tax revenues did not show the expected buoyancy reflecting the sluggishness in industrial production in the first half of the year".

29.1.8 In 1984-85, the revenue deficit increased by Rs. 3497 crores. This deficit was more than 12 per cent of the total revenue expenditure of Rs. 27,881 crores in 1984-85. The Economic Survey for 1984-85 stated as follows:

"Every possibility of raising the balance from current revenues by improving tax collections and effecting saving in current expenditures (e.g. by reducing all non-productive subsidies whether implicit or explicit) would also need to be explored".

29.1.9 The revenue deficit of Rs. 5888 crores in 1985-86 was almost 17 per cent of the total revenue expenditure (Rs. 34,772 crores) of that year. The Economic Survey for 1985-86 stated that following "the recommendations of Eighth Finance Commission, the States' share in the Union excise duties was raised from 40 per cent to 45 per cent. As a result, the growth in the Centre's share in the tax revenue in 1985-86 (BE) was expected to be only ten per cent over 1984-85 (BE), as against a growth of 15.8 per cent in 1984-85 (RE) over the actuals of the preceding year. The growth of non-tax revenues also decelerated from 29.1 per cent in 1984-85 to 21.5 per cent in the current year". Apart from the fact that the revenue receipts were less than expectation, the increase in revenue expenditure (Rs. 6891 crores) over that in 1984-85 was quite heavy.

29.1.10 The revenue deficit further increased to Rs. 7776 crores in 1986-87, which was a little more than 18 per cent of the total revenue expenditure (Rs. 42,544 crores) of that year. The Economic Survey for 1986-87 stated as follows:

"Despite the enviable record in raising revenues, the Government's resource position continued to be under heavy pressure because of the rapid increase in expenditure commitments, especially on non-Plan account. The rapid growth in non-Plan expenditure has meant that the Centre's budget on revenue account has been in deficit throughout this decade and this deficit has increased steadily in the past five years. By 1985-86 (RE), the deficit on revenue account had risen to about 2.4 per cent of GDP. As a result, the Government has had to rely increasingly on borrowed funds to meet its expenditure commitments and this, in turn, has led to a growing bill for interest payments. In 1985-86 (RE) defence, interest payments, and major subsidies accounted for 67 per cent of the Centre's total non-Plan expenditure. In 1986-87, the proportion rose to 70 per cent.

Recognising the gravity of the expenditure problem, the Government undertook a number of measures during the course of the year to strengthen control over expenditure. A system of zero-base budgeting was initiated in the course of the formulation of the budget of all Central Government departments for 1987-88. A system of quarterly budgeting has also been initiated from the current year".

29.1.11 That the measures initiated in 1986-87, as mentioned above, were not able to arrest the growth of revenue deficit was evident from not only the increase in revenue deficit in 1986-87, but also the further increase in deficit in 1987-88. The deficit in 1987-88 was Rs. 9137 crores, which was about 19 per cent of the total revenue expenditure of Rs. 48129 crores in that year. The Economic Survey for 1987-88 stated as follows:

"A disturbing feature of the Centre's budgetary development has been the emergence and widening of the deficit in current account since 1979-80. The deficit as a proportion of GDP at current market prices was only 0.6 per cent in 1979-80 and it reached a level of 2.1 per cent in 1985-86 and 2.5 per cent in 1986-87 (RE)".

The Economic Survey for 1987-88 further stated as follows:

"Although the current revenues, particularly tax revenues

have shown substantial improvement in recent years, from 10.6 per cent in 1984-85 and 11.2 per cent in 1985-86 to 12 per cent of GDP in 1986-87 (RE), current expenditures, too, rose sharply to 12.1 per cent, 13.3 per cent and 14.5 per cent of GDP during these years. Among the major items of expenditure, the growth in interest payments has been most pronounced, from about 2.2 per cent of GDP in mid-eighties (1982-83) to the current level of 3.3 per cent and should be a cause for concern. Subsidies were around 1.8 per cent of GDP after having risen from a level of one per cent in mid-seventies (1976-77)".

29.1.12 In 1988-89, the revenue deficit increased further to Rs. 10,515 crores, which was more than 19 per cent of the total estimated revenue expenditure of Rs. 56,255 crores. According to revised estimate for 1989-90, the revenue deficit (Rs. 12,346 crores) was expected to be about 19 per cent of revenue expenditure of Rs. 67,052 crores. The Economic Survey for 1988-89 observed as follows:

"The widening current account is disturbing in as much as it consumes capital receipts without generating matching assets. The growth in current expenditure has continued to outstrip the growth in current revenues, despite strong growth in the latter".

The Economic Survey for 1988-89 further stated as follows:

"As a proportion of GDP current revenues grew from 9.4 per cent in 1980-81 to 12 per cent in 1987-88. Current expenditure in the same period rose from 10 per cent to 14.6 per cent of GDP. Among major items of expenditure, interest payments have shown a marked growth, from about 2.2 per cent in mid-eighties to 3.4 per cent of GDP in 1987-88. Subsidies, too, grew from 1.3 per cent of GDP in the first half of the 80's to an average of 1.9 per cent during 1985-86 to 1987-88".

29.1.13 The Economic Survey for 1989-90 made the following observations:

"It is matter of great concern that a significant part of the borrowed resources goes towards covering revenue deficit of Government, which is substantially larger than the extent of narrowly defined deficit financing (borrowing from RBI through low cost ad hoc treasury bills). As borrowed resources command higher interest rates, the cost of financing the revenue gap has been on the rise.........."

The Economic Survey for 1989-90 further observed as follows:

"..........Growth in revenue expenditure was, however, far in excess; 19.5 per cent during the period. At the same time, tax revenue grew on an average by 17 per cent in nominal terms. This mis-match between growth in tax revenue and revenue expenditure inevitably resulted in a large and widening revenue deficit during the period. Thus revenue deficit enlarged to 2.8 per cent of GDP in 1988-89 (RE) from 2.1 per cent in 1985-86 and 0.6 per cent in 1980-81. The increasing revenue deficit was largely met from borrowed sources involving higher interest payment liabilities. The diversion of high cost borrowed resources for covering revenue deficit dissipated scarce resource while it ensured no return flow to budget. The consequent destabilising effects have lengthened budgetary imbalances throughout the decade of eighties".

29.2.1 During the period from 1991-92 onwards, i.e. after the financial reforms were started, the revenue deficits were as follows:

Year	Total Revenue receipts (Rs. crores)	Total Revenue expenditure (Rs. crores)	Surplus (Rs. crores)	Deficit (Rs. crores)
1991-92	69,117	85,361	–	16,244
1992-93	77,573	96,147	–	18,574
1993-94	79,650	1,12,366	–	32,716
1994-95	95,549	1,26,578	–	31,029
1995-96	1,14,914	1,44,644	–	29,730
1996-97	1,31,686	1,64,340	–	32,654
1997-98 (RE)	1,45,773	1,89,459	–	43,686
1998-99 (BE)	1,70,300	2,18,368	–	48,068

The above table shows that the revenue deficit increased from Rs. 16,244.00 crores in 1991-92 to Rs. 48,068.00 crores in 1998-99 (B.E); this increase was about 190 per cent. Except for a slight decline in 1994-95 and 1995-96, in all the other years there was substantial increase in revenue deficits.

29.2.2 Some of the observations made in the budget speeches of the Finance Ministers and in the Economic Surveys about revenue deficit are quoted below:

(a) In presenting the interim budget for 1991-92, the then Finance Minister, Shri Yashwant Sinha, had said as follows (paragraphs 3&4):

"the time has come for the Government to share its concerns with the Parliament and the people, in an endeavour to evolve a national consensus. So that the restoration of the health of the economy is perceived as a collective responsibility.

Macro-economic imbalances which have been large and persistent are at the root of the problem. The fiscal deficits of the Government had to be met by borrowing at home. The current account deficits of the economy were inevitable financed by borrowing from abroad. The burden of servicing the accumulated internal and external debt has now become onerous. I need hardly stress that neither the Government nor the economy can live beyond its means for long. The room for manoeuvre, to live on borrowed money or time, has been used up completely. The soft options have been exhausted".

(b) In presenting the final budget for 1991-92, Shri Manmohan Singh had said that the objective should be "to move towards a significant reduction of the revenue deficit".

(c) The Economic Survey for 1992-93 observed as follows (paragraph 2.11) :

"The revenue deficit continues to be at a high level although the actuals for 1991-92 are significantly lower than 1990-91. The pressures on the revenue deficit will remain as long as the Government has to set apart increasing outlays on Rural Development, Agriculture, Health and Education and interest payments continue to show a high growth. The growth in the revenue deficit can be moderated if reasonable returns on the investments in departmental and non-departmental enterprises financed by the Government can be ensured......".

29.2.3 In the budget documents of the recent years observations have been made mainly about fiscal deficit and not on revenue deficit, although the latter is the most important element to be tackled in restoring fiscal health.

29.3.1 One actually lives beyond one's means when one is not able to meet one's consumption expenditure out of one's current income. The same is the case for Government when it is not able to meet its revenue expenditure out of revenue receipts. The corrective measure for avoiding such a situation has been discussed in paragraph 9.2 of my book "*Fundamentals of Government Budgeting in India*" as follows:

"The corrective measure in the case of Government is either adjustment of tax level upwards or economy in revenue expenditure. For obvious reasons, there cannot be unlimited upward revision of tax structure, which has its own adverse reaction in the economy of the country. As a measure of prudent financial policy, a balance is, therefore, required to be struck as to the extent up to which the corrective measure will be by adjustment of tax level and to what extent economy measures will be taken".

29.3.2 The corrective measures discussed above are based on the assumption that return on the investments on capital account would be adequate not only for repayment of borrowed funds but also for payment of interest on loans from Government or dividends on investments in share capital. But in our country even that assumption has not been fulfilled as has been discussed in paragraph 23.

It would, however, appear from the earlier paragraphs that Government is aware of not only of this problem but also other reasons for the mounting revenue deficit and the consequences of meeting revenue expenditure in excess of revenue receipts from borrowed funds.

It will appear from paragraph 29.1.8 that the Government is aware of the need for improving tax collections and effecting saving in current expenditures (e.g. by reducing all non-productive subsidies whether implicit or explicit).

It is quite evident that whatever measures the Government has taken so far have not proved adequate to remedy the situation. Now Government is left with only hard options for correcting the imbalance in its revenue budget.

In the above context, it would be relevant to quote the following from the article of Shri D.H. Pai, Panandikar appearing in the "*Hindustan Times*" (Delhi) dated 27 March 1990 (mentioned in paragraph 26.1.3)

"Revenue deficit is the hardcore of the problem and that has precisely been bypassed. It is not for lack of knowing. It is because it needs tremendous political will to check expenditure particularly on schemes which have the highest demonstration value. Whether it is the employment guarantee scheme or the debt relief to the farmers, the money has to come from revenue account. With no additional incomes to fall back on, revenue deficit goes up resulting in exorbitant increases in public debt without creating a corresponding capacity to repay. The easy way out is to postpone the day of reckoning. Dress up the budget and hide its sharp claws and teeth. Every Finance Minister did it...".

29.3.3 It appeared that the hard reality had perhaps dawned on the Central Government, as indicated in the Finance Minister, Shri Yashwant Sinha's statement in Parliament on 27 December 1990 as follows:

"Today, the soft options stand exhausted. It is now imperative for us to start making the necessary macro-economic adjustments. We should have no illusion that fiscal imbalances accumulated over several years can be eliminated at one stroke. But it is essential that we begin to introduce correctives. Even this will mean hard decisions and difficult choices. If we are to restore the economic health of the nation, we must face reality rather than ignore it....".

29.3.4 Shri Sinha's successor, Shri Manmohan Singh had also said on 24th July 1991, while presenting the final budget for 1991-92 that, "There is no time to lose. Neither the Government nor the economy can live beyond its means year after year. The room for manoeuvre, to live on borrowed money or time, does not exist any more".

29.3.5 The Finance Minister had stated in his speech while presenting the budget for 1992-93 that "...the total allocation for non-Plan expenditure stands at Rs. 84,475 crores, higher by Rs. 4,405 crores compared to the Revised Estimates for 1991-92. But then, as I mentioned earlier, the increase in interest expenditure alone is Rs. 4750 crores. Honourable Members would appreciate that the large requirements for interest and subsidies make it difficult to reduce non-Plan expenditure further and this limits the extent to which the budget can support Plan expenditure....".

In 1992-93 interest (32 per cent) and subsidy (12 per cent) accounted for 44 per cent of total revenue expenditure. In 1998-99 (B.E.), interest (34 per cent) and subsidy (11 per cent) accounted for 45 per cent of total revenue expenditure. In 1992-93, interest (Rs. 31,075.00 crores) and subsidy (Rs. 11,995.00 crores) ate up 55.5 per cent of the revenue receipts. In 1998-99 (B.E.), interest (Rs. 75,000.00 crores) and subsidy (Rs. 24683.00 crores) gobbled up 58.5 per cent of the revenue receipts. It is therefore, quite evident that no effective hard decision has yet been taken to tackle the hardcore of the problem of fiscal imbalance, i.e. revenue deficit.

II

SURPLUS/DEFICIT ON CAPITAL ACCOUNT

30.1.1 The following table shows the surplus or deficit in capital account over the years:

Year	Total Capital receipts (Rs. Crores)	Total Capital expenditure (Rs. Crores)	Surplus (Rs. Crores)	Deficit (Rs. Crores)
1	2	3	4	5
1950-51	105	183	–	78
1960-61	1127	1101	126	–
1970-71	2524	2972	–	448
1974-75	3296	4781	–	1485
1975-76	4697	5950	–	1253
1976-77	5573	6016	–	443
1977-78	5588	6951	–	1363
1978-79	6938	8736	–	1798
1979-80	6125	7864	–	1739
1980-81	9432	10295	–	863
1981-82	10156	11254	–	1098
1982-83	12483	12884	980	40.1
1983-84	15861	14881	–	–
1984-85	17768	18015	–	248
1985-86	16708	16135	573	–
1986-87	18529	19014	–	485
1987-88	22026	18705	3321	–
1988-89	25673	20800	4873	–
1989-90	30020	28698	1320	–
1990-91	38997	31782	7215	–
1991-92	38528	29112	9416	–
1992-93	36178	29916	6262	–
1993-94	55440	33684	21756	–
1994-95	68695	38627	30068	–
1995-96	58338	38415	19923	–
1996-97	61544	42074	19470	–
1997-98 (RE)	96731	53045	43686	–
1998-99 (BE)	1,05,933	57865	48068	–

30.1.2 During the period of our study i.e. 1976-77 to 1998-99 (B.E.), the capital expenditure has increased enormously for planned development. Sh. D. H. Panandikar had stated in his article in '*The Hindustan Times* (Delhi)' of 27 March, 1990 (mentioned in paragraph 26.1.3) that capital expenditure "is the hardware of growth. Cut capital expenditure and the dynamism of the economy will be shattered. Are the hard-earned savings of the people mobilised by government to be spent on debt relief to farmers or subsidies on food and fertilisers? That will deplete savings available for electricity generation or modernisation of ports".

30.1.3 As pointed out in paragraph 29.1.2 during the period of our study from 1976-77 to 1998-99 (BE), there was reduction in capital expenditure in 1979-80, 1985-86 and 1987-88. The surplus in capital account in 1983-84, 1985-86 and 1987-88 onwards every year might have been due to conscious economy measures or due to failure in implementation of various projects to the extent for which funds were provided. Be that what may be, the fact remains that the funds were diverted for revenue expenditure, as would be evident from paragraph 31.1.1 and 31.1.2. The observations of Shri Panandikar are correct in an ideal situation, when capital receipts are gainfully invested.

As pointed out earlier, that has not always happened in this country. The result has been that the return from the investments of borrowed funds has not been satisfactory, contributing to the imbalance in the budgetary position, as has been pointed out in paragraph 23. While it may be advisable to avoid wasteful capital expenditure, none will disagree with Shri Panandikar that borrowed funds should not be saved for meeting revenue expenditure. That is why emphasis should be on proper investment of the borrowed funds avoiding wasteful expenditure. But utilisation of such borrowed funds for meeting revenue expenditure is totally unacceptable.

III

BUDGETARY SURPLUS/DEFICIT

31.1.1 The following table shows the overall surplus/deficit over the years:

(Rs. in Crores)

Year	Total Revenue receipts	Total Capital receipts	Total receipts	Total Revenue expen-diture	Total Capital expen-diture	Total expen-diture	Over-all Surplus	Over-all Deficit
1	2	3	4	5	6	7	8	9
1950-51	406	105	511	347	183	530	–	19
1960-61	877	1127	2004	826	1001	1827	177	–
1970-71	3342	2524	5866	3179	2972	6151	–	285
1974-75	6557	3296	9853	5793	4781	10574	–	721
1975-76	8075	4697	12772	7188	5950	13138	–	366
1976-77	8753	5573	14326	8441	6016	14457	–	131
1977-78	9792	5588	15380	9362	6951	16313	–	933
1978-79	11240	6938	18178	10948	8736	19684	–	1506
1979-80	11340	6125	17465	12034	7864	19898	–	2433
1980-81	12829	9432	22261	14544	10295	24839	–	2578
1981-82	15574	10156	25730	15868	11254	27122	–	1392
1982-83	18091	12483	30574	19346	12884	32230	–	1656
1983-84	20493	15861	36354	22890	14881	37771	–	1417
1984-85	24384	17768	42152	27881	18016	45897	–	3745
1985-86	28884	16708	45592	34772	16135	50907	–	5315
1986-87	34768	18529	53297	42544	19014	61558	–	8261
1987-88	38992	22026	61018	48129	18705	66834	–	5816
1988-89	45740	25673	71413	56255	20800	77055	–	5642
1989-90	54614	30020	84634	66528	28698	95226	–	10592
1990-91	57650	38997	96647	76212	31782	107994	–	11347
1991-92	69117	38528	107645	85361	29112	114473	–	6828

(Contd.)

1	2	3	4	5	6	7	8	9
1992-93	77573	36178	113751	96147	29916	126063	–	12312
1993-94	79650	55440	135090	112366	33684	146050	–	10960
1994-95	95549	68695	164244	126578	38627	165205	–	961
1995-96	114914	58338	173252	144644	38415	183059	–	9807
1996-97	131686	61544	193230	164340	42074	206414	–	13184
1997-98 (RE)	145773	96731	242504	189459	53045	242504	–	Nil
1998-99 (BE)	170300	105933	276233	218368	57865	276233	–	Nil

31.1.2 For easier appreciation the following table gives the break up of overall surplus/deficit into revenue surplus/deficit and that on capital account:

(Rs. in Crores)

Year	Revenue Surplus	Revenue Deficit	Surplus on Capital Account	Deficit on Capital Account	Overall Surplus	Overall Deficit
1	2	3	4	5	6	7
1950-51	59	–	–	78	–	19
1960-61	51	–	126	–	177	–
1970-71	163	–	–	448	–	285
1974-75	764	–	–	1485	–	721
1975-76	887	–	–	1253	–	366
1976-77	312	–	–	443	–	131
1977-78	430	–	–	1363	–	933
1978-79	292	–	–	1798	–	1506
1979-80	–	694	–	1739	–	2433
1980-81	–	1715	–	863	–	2578
1981-82	–	294	–	1098	–	1392
1982-83	–	1255	–	401	–	1656
1983-84	–	2397	980	–	–	1417
1984-85	–	3497	–	248	–	3745
1985-86	–	5888	573	–	–	5315
1986-87	–	7776	–	485	–	8261
1987-88	–	9137	3321	–	–	5816
1988-89	–	10515	4873	–	–	5642
1989-90	–	11914	1320	–	–	10594
1990-91	–	18562	7215	–	–	11347

(Contd.)

1	2	3	4	5	6	7
1991-92	–	16244	9416	–	–	6828
1992-93	–	18574	6262	–	–	12312
1993-94	–	32716	21756	–	–	10960
1994-95	–	31029	30068	–	–	961
1995-96	–	29730	19923	–	–	9807
1996-97	–	32654	19470	–	–	13184
1997-98 (RE)*	–	43686	43686	–	–	–
1998-99 (BE)*	–	48068	48068	–	–	–

* There is no overall deficit in these two years due to the abolition of the system of ad hoc Treasury Bills, vide paragraph 26.2.

32.1.1 The reasons for persisting overall deficit were analysed in the Economic Survey for 1972-73 which stated as follows:

"A scrutiny of the Central budget reveals that if expenditures on Plan, Defence and contractual obligations are kept out, the category of civil expenditure susceptible to economy measures would hardly work out to a little more than 10 per cent of the Central Government's total expenditure on both revenue and capital account. This, however, is not to minimise the need of enforcing utmost economy in the non-essential expenditures of the Government or for that matter even in Plan expenditures. Economies in the latter can be secured through proper screening at the stage of project formulation and more efficient implementation of Plan Schemes".

However, the dilemma faced by Government in enforcing economies was evident from the following observations made in the Economic Survey for 1972-73:

"It is of course a truism that in order to bring down the rate of money supply, resort to deficit financing has to be kept within reasonable limits. The dilemma, however, is that any curtailment of developmental activity is self-defeating; this could only slacken growth which in turn would erode the base of resource mobilisation and thus pile up for the future a fiscal problem of far more serious proportions. Even in respect of non-developmental expenditures, defence preparedness cannot be made to suffer, nor do outlays on contractual obligations (e.g. interest payments, etc.) containing any cushion for securing economies".

This dilemma still persists as will be evident from the figures in the tables in paragraphs 29, 30 and 31 and observations made in the Economic Survey for subsequent years, some of which are reproduced below.

32.1.2 The Economic Survey for 1975-76 observed that "with the price level showing a declining trend under the impact of the various anti-inflationary measures taken since July 1974, the fiscal policy as unfolded in the budget for 1975-76 laid greater emphasis on accelerating the rate of growth of the economy, which had been none too satisfactory in the last four years. The overall strategy evolved to achieve this object was to step up the public sector outlay, particularly in the core sectors such as agriculture, irrigation, fertilisers, power, coal petroleum and shipping and transport and to stimulate domestic savings and channelise these to investment in the desired fields through an appropriate mix of incentives".

In this year revenue surplus increased from Rs. 764 crores in 1974-75 to Rs. 887 crores. The deficit on capital account declined from Rs. 1485 crores in 1974-75 to Rs. 1253 crores. The overall deficit thus declined from Rs. 721 crores in 1974-75 to Rs. 366 crores in 1975-76.

32.1.3 The Economic Survey for 1976-77 emphasised the need for maintaining "price stability with growth". With this end in view, the "budget for 1976-77 provided for a sharp step up in public sector investment outlays" said the Economic Survey for 1976-77. It also stated that "the large investment envisaged in the Annual Plan would be achieved only with a higher rate of domestic savings". In this year, overall deficit declined from Rs. 366 crores in 1975 to Rs. 131 crores, because of the sharp decline in the deficit on capital account from Rs. 1253 crores to Rs. 443 crores despite fall in revenue surplus from Rs. 887 crores to Rs. 312 crores. The decline in revenue surplus was indicative of unhealthy sign, which ultimately led to revenue deficit in 1979-80.

32.1.4 It was stated in the Economic Survey for 1977-78 that budget for 1977-78 was presented "against a backdrop of resurgent inflation and slackening investment activity in the economy." This Economic Survey went on to say that the strategy of the budget "was, therefore, to overcome both these obstacles in the way of the growth of the economy." In this year, there was increase in the overall deficit from Rs. 131 crores in 1976-77 to Rs. 933 crores. Although revenue surplus increased from Rs. 312 crores in 1976-77 to Rs. 430 crores, this increase was offset by increase in the deficit on capital account from Rs. 443 crores in 1976-77 to Rs. 1363 crores in 1977-78.

32.1.5 As regards the budgetary policy for 1978-79, the Economic Survey for that year stated that on the eve of the presentation of the Central Budget "the profile of the economy was such that the resurgent inflation had been controlled and the growth in real output particularly in agriculture was estimated to be a record one. Comfortable foreign exchange reserves and a sufficient stock of food-grains were other favourable factors. In the circumstances, the imperatives for budgetary policy were quite obvious. Foremost among them was to provide adequate fiscal stimuli to the growth of investment and to give a concrete shape to the new design of development by public expenditure policy in the direction of more employment oriented programmes. The second was to continue to maintain price stability". In the Central budget for 1978-79, total expenditure was stepped up to achieve these objectives. The overall deficit increased from Rs. 933 crores in 1977-78 to Rs. 1506 crores in 1978-79 due to increase of deficit on capital account from Rs. 1363 crores in 1977-78 to Rs. 1798 crores and decline in revenue surplus from Rs. 430 crores in 1977-78 to Rs. 292 crores.

32.1.6 In the Economic Survey for 1979-80, the following observations were made; this is the year in which revenue deficit started.

"A noteworthy feature of the Government budgets in the past several years has been large increases in expenditure mainly, but not solely, because of the rapid growth in development expenditure. Total Government expenditure which formed 20.4 per cent of GDP at market prices rose to

29.6 per cent in 1978-79. Significant efforts were also made to raise revenues over this period and tax revenues as well as domestic capital receipts have increased rapidly. Nevertheless the growth in domestic revenues has not been sufficient to finance the increase in expenditure. The draft on foreign resources has also declined significantly. As a consequence, budget-deficits have increased. These pressures have been marked in the past three years".

The provision for expenditure in the budget for 1979-80 was less than the revised estimates of 1978-79, this was stated to be largely due to implementation of the recommendations of the Seventh Finance Commission, according to which the flow of grants to States declined. But the share of the States in the proceeds of the Central taxes and duties increased following the recommendations of the Seventh Finance Commission. The net effect was that the Central Government had to make efforts to mobilise additional resources. But these efforts were of not much effect, as 1979-80 was the first year to have revenue deficit, in addition to the deficit on capital account. Although the deficit on capital account in 1979-80 (Rs. 1739 crores) was marginally lower than that in 1978-79 (Rs. 1798 crores) the overall deficit rose from Rs. 1506 crores in 1978-79 to Rs. 2433 crores in 1979-80 due to the revenue deficit of Rs. 694 crores as against the revenue surplus of Rs. 292 crores in 1978-79.

32.1.7 The Economic Survey for 1980-81 made the following observations: "Fiscal policy in 1980-81 had to maintain a very difficult balance between the need to moderate aggregate demand pressures and to impart a developmental thrust to the economy. While the budget for 1980-81 provides for a 16 per cent increase in the Annual Plan Outlay over the 1979-80 level, it also sought to achieve this with only a limited recourse to financing. However, during the course of the year, the Government was faced with a number of unavoidable items of expenditure including especially additional Central assistance for State Plans and for drought and flood relief. Tax revenues are expected to exceed the budget estimates. Public borrowings may also be higher". It also pointed out that "all out effort at eliminating wasteful expenditure, both under non-plan and plan heads will be necessary to bring about a better balance to the Central and State budgets". Despite the efforts which might have been made, there were deficits both in revenue account and capital account. The revenue deficit in 1980-81 increased sharply to Rs. 1715 crores as against Rs. 694 crores in 1979-80. There was, however, decline in deficit on capital account from Rs. 1739 crores in 1979-80 to Rs. 863 crores in 1980-81. The overall deficit in 1980-81 was thus Rs. 2578 crores as against Rs. 2433 crores in 1979-80.

32.1.8 It was indicated in the Economic Survey for 1981-82 that the budget provision for total expenditure in 1981-82 was 8.4 per cent more than the revised estimate of 1980-81. Of the total expenditure, the non-development expenditure was estimated to rise by 5.5 per cent over the revised estimate of 1980-81. Development expenditure, including Plan outlays of the Centre, was expected to rise by 10.5 per cent over that according to the revised estimate of 1980-81. The Economic Survey also stated that the Central Government "made massive efforts to mobilise additional resources in 1981-82". The revenue deficit declined in 1981-82 to Rs. 294 crores from Rs. 1715 crores in 1980-81, although the deficit on capital account rose from Rs. 863 crores in 1980-81 to Rs. 1098 crores. The overall deficit declined from Rs. 2578 crores in 1980-81 to Rs. 1392 crores in 1981-82.

32.1.9 In 1982-83, the aggregate resources were estimated in the budget to be 22 per cent higher than the budget estimates for 1981-82. On the other hand, the total expenditure, according to the budget estimate for that year, was expected to rise by 20 per cent.

Consequently, a lower deficit was expected. The Economic Survey for 1982-83 pointed out that the fiscal policy in 1982-83 "was directed towards maintaining the tempo of development while avoiding inflationary pressures in the economy" and the budget for 1982-83 "aimed at a substantial step up in Plan expenditure while also providing several incentives for increasing savings and investment in the economy". In 1982-83, the revenue deficit again shot up to Rs. 1255 crores from Rs. 294 crores in 1981-82. The deficit on capital account, however, declined to Rs. 401 crores from Rs. 1098 crores in 1981-82. The overall deficit increased from Rs. 1392 crores in 1981-82 to Rs. 1656 crores in 1982-83.

32.1.10 The Economic Survey for 1983-84 pointed out that the fiscal policy in 1983-84 "continued the thrust of earlier years by offering further stimulus to investment both in the public and the private sectors. The objective was to strengthen the process of growth while keeping inflation under control. The Union Budget for 1983-84 provided for a large increase of 26 per cent in Central Plan expenditure above the original level for the previous year".

The Economic Survey went on to stay that there was "a build up of pressure on the Central Budget in the course of the year. Tax revenues did not show the expected buoyancy reflecting the sluggishness in industrial production in the first half of the year. Small savings collections were better than expected. But, internal resources of the public enterprises, including the Railways, were likely to be adversely affected because of increase in wages and input costs. However to bring about a better balance between resources and expenditure, so as to keep the budgetary deficit within reasonable limit, the Government took various steps in January 1984 to cut both Plan as well as non-Plan expenditures". It went on to point out that the widespread drought experienced during 1982-83 not only affected tax revenues but also necessitated increase in non-development expenditure. In 1983-84, the revenue deficit increased from Rs. 1255 crores in 1982-83 to Rs. 2397 crores. There was however, a surplus of Rs. 980 crores on capital account as against the deficit of Rs. 401 crores in 1982-83. The overall deficit consequently declined to Rs. 1417 crores from Rs. 1656 crores in 1982-83.

32.1.11 The Economic Survey for 1984-85 indicated that the budget for 1984-85, the last year of the Sixth Plan, followed "the strategy initiated in the earlier years of the Plan. Highlights of the 1984-85 Budget were: further measures for resources mobilisation, changes in the income and wealth taxes to provide relief to tax payers and create a better climate for compliance; tightening of tax laws to curb tax evasion and avoidance; widening of the incentives for saving and changes in customs and excise duties to help domestic industries and provide a measure of relief to the common man". According to the budget estimates for 1984-85, the aggregate resources were expected to rise by 19.7 per cent as compared to budget estimates for 1983-84, while aggregate expenditure was expected to rise by 19.3 per cent.

In 1984-85 the revenue deficit increased to Rs. 3497 crores from Rs. 2397 crores in 1983-84. There was deficit of Rs. 248 crores on capital account as compared to a surplus of Rs. 980 crores in the earlier year. Thus the overall deficit increased to Rs. 3745 crores in 1984-85 as compared to Rs. 1417 crores in 1983-84.

32.1.12 According to the Economic Survey for 1985-86, in that year, the resources of the Central Government, according to the budget estimates, grew by 16.7 per cent over 1984-85 as against the growth rate of 18.2 per cent according to the revised estimate of 1984-85. The total expenditure provided in the budget for 1984-85 was 19.3 per cent higher than the expenditure budgeted in 1984-85.

The Economic Survey for 1985-86 contained the following observations:

"The year 1985-86 has seen a successful start to the Seventh Five Year Plan, a number of major policy initiatives were taken to boost economic growth, reinforce anti-poverty programmes, revitalise industry and provide a new direction to fiscal policy. The policy decisions were taken against a background of reassuring economic indicators which show a distinct improvement in the growth of Gross National Product (GNP), buoyancy in revenues and a decline in the rate of inflation".

In 1985-86, the revenue deficit increased to Rs. 5888 crores from Rs. 3497 crores in 1984-85, but there was a surplus of Rs. 573 crores on capital account as compared to a deficit of Rs. 248 crores in 1984-85. The overall deficit increased to Rs. 5315 crores as compared to Rs. 3745 crores in 1984-85.

32.1.13 The Economic Survey for 1986-87 pointed out that as a result of mounting revenue deficits "The Government has had to rely increasingly on borrowed funds to meet its expenditure commitment, and this, in turn, has led to a growing bill for interest payments. In 1985-86 (RE) defence expenditure, interest payments and major subsidies accounted for 67 per cent of the Centre's total non-plan expenditure. In 1986-87 (BE), the proportion rose to 70 per cent".

The Economic Survey for 1986-87 went on to say that the Government undertook a number of measures during 1986-87 like zero-base budgeting and a system of quarterly budgeting. Apart from these measures, following recommendations of the Chakravarty Committee, Government introduced a system of monetary targeting on experimental basis, in consultation with the Reserve Bank of India. The Economic Survey for 1986-87 went on to say that "careful scrutiny and control of expenditure will command the highest priority in the years ahead, if inflationary pressures are to be kept in check. The underlying approach to expenditure control must continue to emphasise the need to prioritise expenditures carefully".

In 1986-87, the revenue deficit increased to Rs. 7776 crores as compared to Rs. 5888 crores in 1985-86. There was deficit of Rs. 485 crores on capital account as compared to a surplus of Rs. 573 crores in 1985-86. The overall deficit of Rs. 8261 crores in 1986-87 was the largest till the budget estimates of 1990-91, except the revised estimates for 1989-90 according to which the overall deficit was Rs. 11750 crores.

32.1.14 The Economic Survey for 1987-88 observed that "although the current revenues, particularly tax revenues have shown substantial improvement in recent years from 10.6 per cent in 1984-85 and 11.2 per cent in 1985-86 to 12.0 per cent of GDP in 1986-87 (RE). Current expenditures too, rose sharply to 12.1 per cent, 13.3 per cent and 14.5 per cent of GDP during these years".

In addition, in the Economic Survey for 1988-89 the

following observations were made:

"The budgetary position of the Central Government in 1987-88 (RE) was marked by a deceleration in the growth in aggregate expenditure and a moderate acceleration in the growth in current receipts (inclusive of internal resources of public sector enterprises) compared with the growth in expenditures and current receipts in 1986-87".

In 1987-88 the revenue deficit increased to Rs. 9137 crores as compared to Rs. 7776 crores in 1986-87. However, there was surplus of Rs. 3321 crores on capital account as compared to the deficit of Rs. 485 crores in 1986-87. Because of the surplus on capital account, the overall deficit decreased from Rs. 8261 crores in 1986-87 to Rs. 5816 crores in 1987-88.

32.1.15 The budgetary position of 1988-89 was described as follows in the Economic Survey for 1989-90.

"The Budgetary position of the Central Government was distinctly worse in 1988-89 (RE) with budgetary deficit hardening to Rs. 7940 crores against the actuals of Rs. 5816 crores in 1987-88 and Rs. 4937 crores in 1985-86. The overall expenditure GDP ratio was over 24 per cent, while the ratio of current revenue (including internal resources of Public Sector Undertakings) to GDP was a mere 13.4 per cent and hence the large gap."

In 1988-89, the revenue deficit was Rs. 10515 crores as compared to Rs. 9137 crores in 1987-88. The surplus on capital account in 1988-89 was Rs. 4873 crores as against Rs. 3321 crores in 1987-88. The overall deficit was Rs. 5642 crores as against Rs. 5816 crores in 1987-88.

32.1.16 The Economic Survey for 1989-90 was critical about the pattern of financing revenue deficit with borrowed funds and also, about the fact that remunerative commercial activities had not been generating adequate return flow by way of dividends and interest. It also pointed out that the interest cost of borrowing in the form of small savings, P.F. etc. had increased in recent years because of near stagnant domestic saving rate. The Economic Survey went on to observe that the "net outcome of this pattern of financing is the emergence of unsavoury budgetary imbalances. Increase in borrowings and deficit financing leads to rise in interest payments, liquidity growth and inflation and pushes expenditures further. Growth in expenditure, in turn, necessitates larger borrowing and deficit financing."

The revised estimates for 1989-90 envisaged that the revenue deficit would increase to Rs. 12436 crores from Rs. 10515 crores in 1988-89 and there would be surplus of only Rs. 686 crores on capital account as against the surplus of Rs. 4873 crores in 1988-89.

32.1.17 As mentioned in the Economic Survey for 1990-91 "the budget for 1990-91 laid stress on limiting the size of the budget deficit through containment of expenditure growth and through better tax compliance." The budget estimates for 1990-91 indicated that both the revenue deficit and surplus on capital account would increase to Rs. 13,032 crores and Rs. 5826 crores respectively; because of the sharp increase in surplus on capital account, the overall deficit was estimated to decrease from Rs. 11750 crores in 1989-90 (RE) to Rs. 7206 crores in 1990-91 (BE).

The Economic Survey for 1990-91 summed up the unsatisfactory fiscal position as follows: "Fiscal imbalance, characterised by unabated pressure on Government expenditure and growing deficits in the budget, has continued to remain the major concern of the Government during the last few years. Persistent and large deficits have serious implications not only for the finances of the Government but also for price stability and economic growth. Such deficits have to be met by borrowings by the Central Government with subsequent obligations for interest payments and debt repayment. At a macro-economic level, fiscal deficits inevitably spill into balance of payments problems and create inflationary pressures in the economy. Fiscal correction and consolidation is, therefore, high on the agenda of the Government".

32.1.18 The Economic Survey for 1991-92 (Part II-Sectoral Development paragraph 2.4) observed as follows:

"Such a fiscal situation has become unsustainable. Interest payments on accumulated debts constitute about 24 per cent of total expenditure of the Central Government. Unless firmly dealt with by checking expenditure and raising revenues, such a situation would result in the absorption of an increasing proportion of Government resources necessitating higher borrowings simply to service the past debts, thus pushing the Government into a debt trap. The unabated growth of Government expenditure, particularly non-plan expenditure, has been the main reason for the country falling into the present fiscal crisis."

32.1.19 The Economic Survey for 1991-92 (Part II-Paragraph 2.3) also observed as follows:

"A more complete measure of macro-economic imbalance used internationally is the concept of gross fiscal deficit, which reckons the total resource gap in terms of excess of total Government expenditure over revenue receipts and grants. This concept fully reflects the indebtedness of Government".

With the introduction of the concept of gross fiscal deficit as the indicator of fiscal imbalance, observations and discussions stopped in the budget documents about the other indicator i.e. revenue deficit. Overall deficit budgetary deficit had become irrelevant with the abolition of the system of monetisation of deficit through ad-hoc treasury bills.

32.1.20 The system of ad-hoc treasury bills to finance the budget deficit was discontinued from 1st April 1997. In presenting the budget for 1997-98 the then Finance Minister Shri P. Chidambaram stated that "..... with the discontinuance of ad-hoc treasury bills and tap treasury bills, and the introduction of ways and means of advances, the concept of Budget Deficit, as currently defined, will lose its relevance either as an indicator of short-term requirement of funds by the Government or the extent of monetisation. Therefore, it is proposed to discontinue the practice of showing the 'Budget Deficit'; instead Gross Fiscal Deficit (GFD) would become the key indicator of deficit". Revenue Deficit, however, remains key indicator of the fiscal balance.

IV

GROSS FISCAL DEFICIT

33.1.1 The gross fiscal deficit has been defined as follows in the key to the budget documents, 1999-2000:

"The difference between total expenditure of Government by way of revenue, capital and loans net of repayments on the one hand and revenue receipts of Government and capital receipts which are not in the nature of borrowing but which finally accrue to Government on the other, constitutes gross fiscal deficit".

33.1.2 The following table shows the amounts of gross fiscal deficit from 1990-91 onwards:

Year	Gross Fiscal Deficit (Rs. Crores)
1990-91	44,632
1991-92	36,323
1992-93	40,173
1993-94	60,257
1994-95	57,704
1995-96	60,243
1996-97	66,733
1997-98 (RE)	86,345
1998-99 (BE)	91,025

The above table shows that there was marginal decline in fiscal deficit in 1991-92 and 1994-95. But the fiscal deficit in 1998-99 B.E., (Rs. 91,025.0 crores) was 104 per cent more than that in 1990-91 (Rs. 44,632.0 crores). In 1993-94 and 1997-98 (RE), the fiscal deficit increased sharply by 50 per cent and 30 per cent respectively as compared to each preceding year. In 1992-93, 1995-96, 1996-97 and 1997-98 (RE), fiscal deficit increased by 11 per cent, 4 per cent,

11 per cent and 5 per cent respectively, as compared to each preceding year.

31.1.3. Since 1990-91, gross fiscal deficit, as per cent of GDP (Gross Domestic Product) was as follows:

Year	Fiscal Deficit as per cent of GDP
1990-91	7.7
1991-92	5.9
1992-93	5.7
1993-94	7.5
1994-95	5.6
1995-96	4.9
1996-97	4.7
1997-98 (RE)	5.5
1998-99 (BE)	5.1

These figures as per cent of GDP keep changing, perhaps because of the changes in the figures of GDP. For example, the figures for 1990-91 was 8.3 in the Economic Surveys for 1995-96 and 1996-97. In the Economic Survey for 1998-99, the figure for 1990-91 is 7.7. Similarly, the figure for 1994-95 was 7.4 in the Economic Survey for 1996-97, but the same has been shown as 7.5 in the Economic Survey for 1998-99. In this connection paragraph 53 may please be seen.

33.2.1 Some of the observations in the budget documents about fiscal deficit are reproduced below:

(a) The Economic Survey for 1993-94 stated as follows (paragraphs 46 to 50):

"As we approach the end of 1993-94 it is clear that the Centre's fiscal deficit is significantly larger than budgeted and inflationary potential is building. Thus far the fiscal pressures on inflation and the balance of payments have been offset by the unused capacity in industry (due to slow recovery) and the contractionary influences of long overdue financial sector reform. But these offsetting forces can be expected to weaken over time and it is vital to reassert control over the fiscal situation to curb inflation, reduce interest rates, release resources for productive investment and sustain confidence in the economy.

Returning to a medium-term path of fiscal deficit contraction will entail serious changes in both expenditure and revenue policies. The key issues in expenditure policy relate to the control of major subsidies and effective prioritisation of discretionary expenditures. In a poor country some subsidy on basic foodgrain is justified. But our present large and burgeoning food subsidy is poorly targetted and wasteful. In the short-run, containment of the food subsidy requires moderation in procurement price increases, prompt adjustment of issue prices and cost reduction in Food Corporation of India operation. In the medium-term, it is essential to move to a system where the subsidy is confined to the deserving poorest sections of society and delivery costs are reduced. One possibility is to shift to a programme of food stamps for the poor. Another is to decentralize much of the procurement-distribution function of the Food Corporation of India and the Centre to the States and these organisations, with the objectives of achieving greater efficiency, accountability, improved targetting and subsidy reduction.

Similarly, the present large and growing subsidy on urea cannot be sustained indefinitely. The existing low prices for nitrogenous fertilizers relative to phosphatic and potash are encouraging use of inappropriate mixes, with serious potential harm to soil fertility and agriculture. Quite apart from any revision in urea prices, the system of plant-specific retention prices for urea producers encourages wasteful use of capital and energy and discourages cost saving. It is not in the long-run interests of farmers and should be replaced, over time, by a modest protective tariff combined with a subsidy targetted at small farmers.

Effective prioritisation of expenditure requires that limited resources be focussed on completing ongoing projects rather than starting new ones. There has been a proliferation of under-funded projects, resulting in increasing time and cost over-runs, as limited resources are spread too thinly. The greatest benefits can now accrue from speedily completing unfinished projects. Low user charges on existing projects and programmes inevitably results in non-availability of funds for maintenance and upkeep and for additions and expansions. The quality of output or service provided by the completed project, therefore, deteriorates over time. To ensure greater benefits from costly assets like irrigation and power, more effective strategies for pricing and cost recovery are vital to cover operation and maintenance costs and contribute towards financing expansions. Expenditure prioritisation and control should also be sought through systematic zero-based budgeting procedures, whereby existing programmes are evaluated and low priority expenditures pruned.

Fiscal deficit control also requires measures to raise revenues. Broadening of the domestic direct and indirect tax base, is a critical component of the strategy for revenue generation and reduction of rates to moderate levels. A competitive industrial structure and sustained export growth requires a phased shift in the overall tax structure from customs to broad-based domestic taxes. The ratio of customs to total revenues in India is much higher than in competitor developing countries and is a serious impediment to our international competitiveness. A broadening of the domestic tax base is, therefore, critical to the achievement of deficit and tax reform objectives".

(b) In presenting the budget for 1994-95, the Finance Minister Shri Manmohan Singh had stated as follows (paragraphs 6 & 7):

In real life the picture is never entirely rosy and there are some warning signals which we must heed. It has not been possible to contain the fiscal deficit in the current year to the level we had originally targetted. The slower pace of industrial recovery in 1993-94 led to a shortfall in revenues and various expenditures have also exceeded Budget estimates. The slippage in the fiscal deficit in 1993-94 has been less damaging than might have been the case ordinarily, mainly because of the existence of sizeable idle industrial capacity and low investment levels. But as investment begins to revive, we cannot afford continuing weakness on the fiscal front. Unless the deterioration witnessed in the current year is speedily reversed, there is a serious danger that we may slip back into a position where large government deficits fuel inflation, widen the current account imbalance and push up interest rates, making it impossible to bring about the rapid economic growth we need to raise living standards and create productive jobs in adequate numbers.

In formulating this Budget, I have sought to address six major tasks:

- First , we must accelerate the reform and modernisation of our tax system we began two years ago
- Second, we must correct the slippage in the fiscal deficit that has occurred in the current year.
- Third, we must build on the demonstrable success already achieved in the external sector where our strong performance has vindicated our strategy of phased integration with the world economy.
- Fourth, the Budget must provide a major stimulus for a strong industrial recovery, especially for investment and capital goods production.
- Fifth, and most importantly, we must reorient our development policies and programmes to address more effectively the problems of poverty, unemployment and social deprivation which affect a large mass of our people, particularly in rural areas.
- Sixth, we have to consolidate and deepen the progress we have made in restoring the health of our banking system.

(c)The Economic Survey for 1995-96 observed as follows (paragraph 12):

"The declining trend of fiscal deficit which suffered a temporary reversal in 1993-94 has been again restored and strengthened further. From 7.5 per cent of GDP in 1993-94, the fiscal deficit declined to 6.5 per cent in 1994-95 (RE) (Table 2.1). The fiscal deficit would have been still lower but for sudden surge in the collection from Small Savings and resultant increase in the loans to States and Union Territories. These loans are treated as expenditure of the Central Government and add to the fiscal deficit. If this expenditure, over which the Central Government has no control, is excluded, the fiscal deficit declines to 5.4 per cent of GDP".

(d) The Economic Survey for 1996-97 stated as follows (paragraph 1)

" The Budget for 1996-97 continued the process of fiscal adjustment within the framework of the Common Minimum Programme (CMP). The budget has envisaged fiscal correction of 0.8 per cent point through a reduction in the gross fiscal deficit (GFD) as a proportion of GDP from 5.8 per cent in 1995-96 (RE) to 5 per cent in 1996-97 (BE). Also the primary deficit as a proportion of GDP is budgeted to fall to 0.2 per cent of GDP. The other dimension of the gross fiscal adjustment is its quality as reflected in the composition of fiscal adjustment. The compression in the fiscal deficit during the current year has been attempted through a combination of an increase in revenue coupled with reduction in expenditure. Revenue receipts as a proportion of GDP are budgeted to edge upwards from 10.0 per cent in 1995-96 (RE) to 10.4 per cent in 1996-97. On the other hand, revenue expenditure as a proportion of GDP is expected to decline from 13.1 per cent in 1995-96 (RE) to 12.9 per cent in 1996-97 (BE). This is largely on account of containment of non-interest non-plan expenditure".

(e) The Economic Survey for 1998-99 stated as follows (paragraphs 11 & 12):

"The gross fiscal deficit is defined as the difference between revenue receipts (net) plus non-debt capital receipts and the total expenditure including loans net of repayments. This is a measure, which captures the entire shortfall in the non-debt resources for financing the Central Government operations. The fiscal deficit as a proportion of GDP at current market prices for 1997-98 is now placed at 5.5 per cent and is still larger than the budgeted target of 4.2 per cent for 1997-98. The budget for 1998-99 targeted the fiscal deficit at 5.6 per cent of GDP which is now placed at 5.1 per cent based on the latest GDP estimates. The revenue deficit, which indicates the extent of borrowing required to finance current expenditure, was budgeted at Rs. 48,068 crores (2.7 per cent of GDP) compared with Rs. 43,686 crores (2.8 per cent of GDP) for 1997-98 (RE). The primary deficit, which is an indicator of current fiscal operations of the Central Government, was estimated at Rs. 16,025 crores (0.9 per cent of GDP) for 1998-99 compared with Rs. 20,645 crores (1.3 per cent of GDP) attained in 1997-98 (RE).

The fiscal adjustment envisaged in 1998-99 is sought through a combination of mobilisation of additional resources and containment of expenditure".

PART V – ACCURACY IN BUDGETING

I

ACCURACY IN BUDGETING

34.1.1 Accuracy is of utmost importance in making estimates of resources and their application. This has been emphasised in paragraph 23.1.1 of my book "*Fundamentals of Government Budgeting in India*" as follows:

"Accuracy is the *sine qua non* for making estimates for budget provision for any financial year. It is true that estimates can never be hundred per cent accurate, but it is essential that the estimates are as near as possible to actual realisation/requirements. Overestimation of resources may result in undesirable tax concessions or provisions for avoidable expenditure. On the other hand, underestimation of resources may result in unnecessary tax burden or curtailment of high priority developmental activity. Underestimation of expenditure on some items may also result in undesirable tax concessions or provision for items of lesser priority. Both overestimation of resources and underestimation of expenditure may ultimately result in unanticipated budget deficit or larger deficit than contemplated, with consequential adverse effect on economy of the country. Each estimating authority has, therefore, to keep these factors in mind in formulating its budget proposal."

34.1.2 No norms of accuracy for Government budgeting have been laid down. It is difficult to lay down norms of accuracy in Government budgeting; there are many imponderables, particularly in a country like India where Government budgets are subject to vagaries of weather to a large extent. It is also not possible to prescribe how the desired accuracy can be achieved. This has been dealt with in paragraph 23.1.3 of my book "*Fundamentals of Government*

Budgeting in India" quoted below:

"It is not possible to define how the desired accuracy can be achieved. The most basic principle that the estimating authority has to follow in estimating the resources and their application is that it should apply the same prudence which an ordinary individual will apply in planning his own expenditure keeping in view his resource position".

34.1.3 The Comptroller and Auditor General of India makes a comparison of the budget estimates with the actuals relating to each financial year in his Audit Report. So far as the figures of receipts are concerned, comparison made by him is with reference to the budget estimates and the actuals appearing in the accounts. However, there is a difference in respect of figures of expenditure. As mentioned in paragraph 7.5.2 of my book "*Fundamentals of Government Budgeting in India*", the figures in the Annual Financial statement are net figures (i.e. after reduction in respect of receipts which are taken in reduction of expenditure). This is why the demands for grants are prepared for gross expenditure for obtaining vote of Parliament, vide paragraph 13.2 of my book "*Fundamentals of Government Budgeting in India*".

The comparison made by the Comptroller and Auditor General of India is between the gross amount so voted and actual expenditure (gross) appearing in accounts. This comparison of gross actual expenditure figures as per accounts with those voted by Parliament is essential for meeting the requirement of Article 115 of the Constitution of India, according to which if there is excess expenditure over the amount voted against any particular demand for grant, fresh approval of the Parliament is necessary for the excess expenditure through another demand for grant. These aspects have been dealt with in paragraph 28 of my book "*Fundamentals of Government Budgeting in India*".

34.1.4 For our limited purpose of merely testing the accuracy in budget estimates, we may compare the estimated net figures as per budget with the actual figures of both net receipts and net expenditure as per the accounts.

34.2.1 The following table shows the comparative position of actual revenue receipts, the revenue expenditure and revenue surplus/deficit as compared to the budget estimates.

REVENUE ACCOUNT

Year	Revenue receipts			Revenue Expenditure			Surplus/Deficit		
	Bud. Rs. Cr.	Act. Rs. Cr.	Variation %	Bud. Rs. Cr.	Act. Rs. Cr.	Variation %	Bud. Rs. Cr.	Act. Rs. Cr.	Variation %
1	2*	3*	4	5*	6*	7	8*	9*	10
75-76	7092	8075	+14	6491	7188	+13	+601	+887	+47
76-77	8227	8752	+6	7690	8440	+10	+537	+312	-42
77-78	9541	9792	+3	9737	9362	-4	-196	+430	-319
78-79	10812	11240	+4	10958	10948	-0.1	-146	+292	-300
79-80	11182	11339	+1	11396	12033	+6	-214	-694	+224
80-81	12327	12829	+4	14256	14544	+2	-1929	-1715	-11
81-82	14327	15574	+9	15299	15868	+4	-972	-294	-70
82-83	17595	18091	+3	18227	19345	+6	-632	-1254	+99
83-84	20625	20493	-0.6	22419	22890	+2	-1794	-2397	+34
84-85	24016	24384	+2	26342	27881	+5	-2326	-3497	+50
85-86	27084	29207	+8	32718	34772	+6	-5634	-5565	-1
86-87	31400	34768	+11	38274	42544	+11	-6874	-7776	+13
87-88	38202	38992	+2	44945	48129	+7	-6743	-9137	+37

Surplus + Variation +Increase in Surplus/Deficit

Deficit - Variation - Decrease in Surplus/Deficit

* *Source* : Reports on Currency and Finance of Reserve Bank of India.

34.2.2 It will appear from the above table that in 1983-84, there was the smallest variation between budget estimate and actual of revenue receipts in the years under review. The variation was minus 0.6 per cent, i.e. the actual revenue receipts were less than the budget estimate by 0.6 per cent. In that year, revenue expenditure, however, exceeded the budget estimate by 2 per cent only. Nevertheless, the combined effect of the lesser revenue receipt of 0.6 per cent, and more expenditure by 2 per cent, as compared to the respective budget estimate, was that the revenue deficit exceeded the budget estimate by 34 per cent.

34.2.3 In 1979-80, actual revenue receipts exceeded the budget estimate by one per cent. In that year, the actual revenue expenditure exceeded the budget by 6 per cent. The net result was that the actual revenue deficit of that year exceeded the budget estimate by 224 per cent.

34.2.4 In 1984-85 and 1987-88, the actual revenue receipt exceeded the budget estimate of the respective year by 2 per cent. In 1984-85, the actual revenue expenditure exceeded the budget estimate by 5 per cent, resulting in increase in revenue deficit by 50 per cent. In 1987-88, the revenue expenditure exceeded the budget estimate by 7 per cent, resulting in increase in revenue deficit by 37 per cent.

34.2.5 In 1977-78 and 1982-83, the actual revenue receipts exceeded the budget estimate of the respective year by 3 per cent. In 1977-78, the revenue expenditure was less by 4 per cent than the budget estimate and in that year as against the estimated revenue deficit of Rs. 196 crores, there was a revenue surplus of Rs. 430 crores accounting for a variation of 319 per cent. In 1982-83, the actual revenue expenditure exceeded the budget estimate by 6 per cent accounting for an increase of 99 per cent in revenue deficit.

34.2.6 The actual revenue receipts exceeded the budget estimate of the respective year by 4 per cent in 1978-79 and 1980-81. In 1978-79, the actual revenue expenditure was less than the budget estimate by only 0.1 per cent (lowest variation in the period from 1975-76 to 1987-88) which resulted in the estimated deficit of Rs. 146 crores, as per the budget, turning into a surplus of Rs. 292 crores, accounting for a variation of 300 per cent. In 1980-81 the actual revenue expenditure exceeded the budget estimate by 2 per cent resulting in a deficit which was lower by 11 per cent as compared to the budget estimate.

34.2.7 In 1976-77, the actual revenue receipts exceeded the budget estimates by 6 per cent. The actual revenue expenditure was, however, 10 per cent more than the budget estimates. The estimate of revenue surplus was Rs. 537 crores according to the budget estimates of 1976-77. The actual revenue surplus (Rs. 312 crores) was 42 per cent less.

34.2.8 In 1985-86, the actual revenue receipts were 8 per cent more than the budget estimates. The actual revenue expenditure exceeded the budget estimates by 6 per cent.

The actual revenue deficit was less by one per cent than the estimated revenue deficit as per budget.

34.2.9 The actual revenue receipt in 1981-82 was 9 per cent more than the budget estimate. The actual revenue expenditure exceeded the budget estimate by 4 per cent. The net effect was that the actual revenue deficit was less by 70 per cent than the budget estimate.

34.2.10 In 1986-87, the increase in actual revenue receipts was 11 per cent as compared to the budget estimate. The same was the increase in actual revenue expenditure as compared to budget estimate. The actual revenue deficit was, as a result, 13 per cent more than the budget estimate.

34.2.11 The increase in actual revenue receipt was 14 per cent more in 1975-76 than the budget estimate. The actual revenue expenditure was more than the budget estimate by 13 per cent. In terms of percentage, the variations in respect of both revenue receipts and revenue expenditure were maximum in this year. The revenue surplus was 47 per cent more than the budget estimate in this year.

35.1.1 The variations in actual capital receipts and actual capital expenditure as compared to the respective budget estimates for each year during 1975-76 to 1987-88 are shown in the table below:

CAPITAL ACCOUNT

Year	Receipts on Capital Accounts			Expenditure on Capital Account			Surplus/Deficit		
	Bud. Rs. Cr.	Act. Rs. Cr.	Variation %	Bud. Rs. Cr.	Act. Rs. Cr.	Variation %	Bud. Rs. Cr.	Act. Rs. Cr.	Variation %
1	2(*)	3(*)	4	5(*)	6(*)	7	8(*)	9(*)	10
'75-76	3951	4697	+19	4799	5950	+24	-848	-1253	+48
'76-77	5089	5573	+10	5946	6016	+1	-857	-443	-48
'77-78	6755	5586	-17	7174	6951	-3	-419	-1363	+225
'78-79	7199	6938	-4	8590	8736	+2	-1391	-1798	+29
'79-80	6655	6125	-8	7823	7864	+0.5	-1168	-1739	+49
'80-81	9877	9432	-5	9394	10294	+10	+483	-862	-278
'81-82	9712	10156	+5	10279	11254	+9	-567	-1098	+94
'82-83	11072	13286	+20	11810	13687	+16	-738	-401	-46

(Contd.)

1	2(*)	3(*)	4	5(*)	6(*)	7	8(*)	9(*)	10
'83-84	13451	15861	+18	13212	14881	+13	+239	+980	+310
'84-85	17717	17768	+0.3	17154	18016	+5	+563	-248	-144
'85-86	20863	16763	-20	18578	16135	-13	+2285	+628	-73
'86-87	24897	18529	-26	21673	19014	-12	+3224	-485	-115
'87-88	20566	22026	+7	19512	18705	-4	+1054	+3321	+215

Surplus + Variation +Increase in Surplus/Deficit
Deficit - Variation - Decrease in Surplus/Deficit

(*) *Source* : Reports on Currency and Finance of Reserve Bank of India.

35.1.2 The smallest variation in actual capital receipts as compared to budget estimates was in 1984-85, in which year the actual receipts exceeded the budget estimate by 0.3 per cent. In that year actual capital expenditure exceeded the budget by 5 per cent. The net effect was that there was actual deficit of Rs. 248 crores as against the surplus of Rs. 563 crores in the budget estimate accounting for a variation of 144 per cent.

35.1.3 In 1978-79, actual capital receipts were less than the budget estimate by 4 per cent. The actual capital expenditure exceeded the budget estimate by 2 per cent. The deficit on capital account increased consequently by 29 per cent.

35.1.4 In 1980-81, the actual capital receipts fell short of the budget estimate by 5 per cent. The actual capital expenditure, however, exceeded the budget estimate by 10 per cent. The estimated surplus of Rs. 483 crores in the budget estimate turned into a deficit of Rs. 862 crores, accounting for a variation of 278 per cent.

35.1.5 In 1981-82, the actual capital receipts exceeded the budget estimate by 5 per cent, while the actual capital expenditure was 9 per cent more than the budget estimate. The actual deficit exceeded the estimated deficit in budget by 94 per cent.

35.1.6 In 1987-88, the actual capital receipts exceeded the budget estimate by 7 per cent. On the other hand, the actual expenditure on capital account was 4 per cent less than the budget estimate. The actual surplus on capital account thus exceeded the budget estimate by 215 per cent.

35.1.7 The actual capital receipts in 1979-80 were less by 8 per cent than the budget estimate. The variation between the actual capital expenditure and budget estimate was the lowest in that year; the actual capital expenditure exceeded the budget estimate by 0.5 per cent. The deficit on capital account exceeded the budget estimate by 49 per cent.

35.1.8 In 1976-77, the actual capital receipts exceeded the budget estimate by 10 per cent. In that year the capital expenditure exceeded the budget estimate by merely one per cent. The actual deficit on capital account consequently was less than the budget estimate by 48 per cent.

35.1.9 The actual capital receipts in 1977-78 were 17 per cent less than the budget estimate and the actual capital expenditure was also less than the budget estimate by 3 per cent. As a result, the actual deficit on capital account exceeded the budget estimate by 225 per cent.

35.1.10 The increase in the amount of actual capital receipts in 1983-84 was 18 per cent as compared to the budget estimate, while the increase in actual capital expenditure was 13 per cent as compared to the budget estimate. The actual surplus on capital account thus exceeded the budget estimate by 310 per cent.

35.1.11 In 1975-76, the actual capital receipts exceeded the budget estimate by 19 per cent. In that year, the variation in actual capital expenditure as compared to the budget estimate was the maximum in the period under review; the capital expenditure exceeded the budget estimate by 24 per cent. This resulted in increase of actual deficit on capital account by 48 per cent over the budget estimate.

35.1.12 The actual capital receipts in 1982-83 exceeded the budget estimate by 20 per cent. The increase in actual capital expenditure as compared to budget estimate was 16 per cent. The actual deficit on capital account was less than the budget estimate by 46 per cent.

35.1.13 In 1985-86, the actual capital receipts were less than the budget estimate by 20 per cent. In that year, the actual capital expenditure was also 13 per cent less than the budget estimate. The actual surplus on capital account was thus 73 per cent less than the budget estimate.

35.1.14 In 1986-87, the variation between the actual capital receipts and the budget estimate was the maximum; the actual capital receipts were 26 per cent less than the budget estimate. The actual capital expenditure was also 12 per cent less than the budget estimate. There was thus deficit of Rs. 485 crores as against surplus of Rs. 3224 crores estimated in the budget, accounting for a variation of 115 per cent.

35.1.15 The effect of variations in revenue surplus/deficit and surplus/deficit on capital account on overall surplus/deficit will be evident from the table below:

Year	Revenue Surplus/Deficit			Surplus/Deficit on Capital Account			Overall Surplus/Deficit		
	Bud. Rs. Cr.	Act. Rs. Cr.	Variation %	Bud. Rs. Cr.	Act. Rs. Cr.	Variation %	Bud. Rs. Cr.	Act. Rs. Cr.	Variation %
1	2	3	4	5	6	7	8	9	10
'75-76	+601	+887	+47	-848	-1253	+48	-247	-366	+47
'76-77	+537	+312	-42	-857	-443	-48	-330	-131	-60
'77-78	-196	+430	-319	-419	-1363	+225	-615	-933	+52
'78-79	-146	+292	-300	-1391	-1798	+29	-1537	-1506	-2
'79-80	-214	-694	+224	-1168	-1739	+49	-1382	-2433	+79
'80-81	-1929	-1715	-11	+483	-862	-278	-1446	-2577	+78
'81-82	-972	-294	-70	-567	-1098	+94	-1539	-1392	-10
'82-83	-632	-1254	+99	-738	-401	-46	-1370	-1655	+21
'83-84	-1794	-2397	+34	+239	+980	+310	-1555	-1417	-9
'84-85	-2326	-3497	+50	+563	-248	-144	-1753	-3745	+114
'85-86	-5634	-5565	-1	+2285	+628	-73	-3349	-4937	+47
'86-87	-6874	-7776	+13	+3224	-485	-115	-3650	-8261	+132
'87-88	-6743	-9137	+37	+1054	+3321	+215	-5689	-5816	+2

Surplus + Variation +Increase in Surplus/Deficit
Deficit - Variation - Decrease in Surplus/Deficit

36. In 1995-96, the actuals varied with the budget estimates as follows:

	Budget (Rs. Crores)	Actual (Rs. Crores)	Variation (per cent)
Revenue Receipts	1,06,462	1,14,914	+8
Revenue Expenditure	1,42,003	1,44,644	+2
Deficit	35,541	29,730	-2
Capital Receipts	66,364	58,330	-12
Capital Expenditure	35,823	38,415	+7
Surplus	30,541	19,923	-35

It would appear from the above figures that the actuals did not vary with budget estimates in 1995-96 as widely as in earlier years up to 1987-88.

37.1.1 From the details given in paragraphs 34, 35 and 36, it will be clear how difficult it is to lay down any norm of accuracy in budgeting. To clarify the point further, illustrations are given below with reference to the figures of budget estimates and actuals of 1987-88, indicating how the revenue surplus/deficit is affected with one per cent variation either in revenue receipts or revenue expenditure or in both; the figures of actuals are assumed actuals with variation of one per cent or no variation.

(i) One per cent increase in revenue receipts without any variation in revenue expenditure.

(Rs. in Crores)

Revenue receipts		Revenue expenditure		Surplus/Deficit		
Budget	Actual	Budget	Actual	Budget	Actual	Variation
28202	38584	44945	44945	-6743	-6361	-6%

(ii) One per cent increase in both revenue receipts and revenue expenditure.

(Rs. in Crores)

Revenue receipts		Revenue expenditure		Surplus/Deficit		
Budget	Actual	Budget	Actual	Budget	Actual	Variation
38202	38584	44945	45394	-6743	-6810	+1 %

(iii) No variation in revenue receipts and one per cent increase in revenue expenditure.

(Rs. in Crores)

Revenue receipts		Revenue expenditure		Surplus/Deficit		
Budget	Actual	Budget	Actual	Budget	Actual	Variation
38202	38202	44945	45394	-6743	-7192	+7 %

(iv) One per cent increase in revenue receipts and one per cent decrease in revenue expenditure.

(Rs. in Crores)

Revenue receipts		Revenue expenditure		Surplus/Deficit		
Budget	Actual	Budget	Actual	Budget	Actual	Variation
38202	38584	44945	44496	-6743	-5912	-12 %

(v) One per cent decrease in revenue receipts and one per cent increase in revenue expenditure.

(Rs. in Crores)

Revenue receipts		Revenue expenditure		Surplus/Deficit		
Budget	Actual	Budget	Actual	Budget	Actual	Variation
38202	37820	44945	45394	-6743	-7574	+12 %

(vi) One per cent decrease in both revenue receipts and revenue expenditure.

(Rs. in Crores)

Revenue receipts		Revenue expenditure		Surplus/Deficit		
Budget	Actual	Budget	Actual	Budget	Actual	Variation
38202	37820	44945	44496	-6743	-6676	-1 %

(vii) One per cent decrease in revenue receipts with no change in revenue expenditure.

(Rs. in Crores)

Revenue receipts		Revenue expenditure		Surplus/Deficit		
Budget	Actual	Budget	Actual	Budget	Actual	Variation
38202	37820	44945	44945	-6743	-7125	+6 %

(viii) No change in revenue receipts and one per cent decrease in revenue expenditure.

(Rs. in Crores)

Revenue receipts		Revenue expenditure		Surplus/Deficit		
Budget	Actual	Budget	Actual	Budget	Actual	Variation
38202	38202	44945	44496	-6743	-6294	-7 %

37.1.2 It will appear from the above that one per cent variation with budget estimate either in revenue receipts or revenue expenditure or both causes increase or decrease in the revenue deficit between one and twelve per cent.

When both revenue receipts and revenue expenditure increase by 1 per cent the deficit increases by Rs. 67 crores, while one per cent decrease in both revenue receipts and revenue expenditure decreases the deficit by the same amount.

If revenue receipts increase by one per cent, without any

variation in revenue expenditure, the revenue deficit decreases by Rs. 382 crores and increases by the same amount when there is a decrease of one per cent in revenue receipts with no change in revenue expenditure.

With revenue receipts remaining unaltered, the revenue deficit increases by Rs. 449 crores if the revenue expenditure increases by one per cent and decreases by the same amount, if the revenue receipts remain unaltered but the revenue expenditure decreases by one per cent.

If there is one per cent increase in revenue receipts and one per cent decrease in revenue expenditure, the revenue deficit decreases by Rs. 831 crores, while if revenue receipts decrease by one per cent the revenue deficit increases by Rs. 831 crores.

In other words, with one per cent variation in either revenue receipts or revenue expenditure or in both, the revenue deficit may increase or decrease by Rs. 67 crores, Rs. 382 crores, as Rs. 449 crores and Rs. 831 crores in the different situations indicated earlier.

38.1.1 Similarly, the surplus/deficit on capital account in 1987-88 may vary in the following manner if there is one per cent variation either in capital receipt or capital expenditure or in both; the figures of 'actual' in the tables below are assumed figures with one per cent variation or no variation.

(i) One per cent increase in capital receipts without any variation in capital expenditure.

(Rs. in Crores)

Capital receipts		Capital expenditure		Surplus/Deficit on capital account		
Budget	Actual	Budget	Actual	Budget	Actual	Variation
20566	20772	19512	19512	+1054	+1260	+20 %

(ii) One per cent increase in both capital receipts and capital expenditure.

(Rs. in Crores)

Capital receipts		Capital expenditure		Surplus/Deficit on capital account		
Budget	Actual	Budget	Actual	Budget	Actual	Variation
20566	20772	19512	19707	+1054	+1065	+1 %

(iii) No variation in capital receipts and one per cent increase in capital expenditure.

(Rs. in Crores)

Capital receipts		Capital expenditure		Surplus/Deficit on capital account		
Budget	Actual	Budget	Actual	Budget	Actual	Variation
20566	20566	19512	19707	+1054	+859	-19 %

(iv) One per cent increase in capital receipts and one per cent decrease in capital expenditure.

(Rs. in Crores)

Capital receipts		Capital expenditure		Surplus/Deficit on capital account		
Budget	Actual	Budget	Actual	Budget	Actual	Variation
20566	20772	19512	19317	+1054	+145	+38 %

(v) One per cent decrease in capital receipts and one per cent increase in capital expenditure.

(Rs. in Crores)

Capital receipts		Capital expenditure		Surplus/Deficit on capital account		
Budget	Actual	Budget	Actual	Budget	Actual	Variation
20566	20360	19512	19707	+1054	+653	-38 %

(vi) One per cent decrease in both capital receipts and capital expenditure.

(Rs. in Crores)

Capital receipts		Capital expenditure		Surplus/Deficit on capital account		
Budget	Actual	Budget	Actual	Budget	Actual	Variation
20566	20360	19512	19317	+1054	+1043	-1 %

(vii) One per cent decrease in capital receipts with no change in capital expenditure.

(Rs. in Crores)

Capital receipts		Capital expenditure		Surplus/Deficit on capital account		
Budget	Actual	Budget	Actual	Budget	Actual	Variation
20566	20360	19512	19512	+1054	+848	-20 %

(viii) No change in capital receipts and one per cent decrease in capital expenditure.

(Rs. in Crores)

Capital receipts		Capital expenditure		Surplus/Deficit on capital account		
Budget	Actual	Budget	Actual	Budget	Actual	Variation
20566	20566	19512	19317	+1054	+1249	+19 %

38.1.2 The details worked out above show that one per cent variation in capital receipts or capital expenditure or in both results in increase or decrease of surplus, as compared to that in budget, varying between 1 per cent and 38 per cent.

One per cent increase in both capital receipts and capital expenditure increases the surplus by Rs. 11 crores as compared to the budget estimate while one per cent decrease in both capital receipt and capital expenditure decreases the same by Rs. 11 crores.

With no variation in capital receipts and one per cent increase in capital expenditure the surplus decreases by Rs. 195 crores, as compared to the budget estimate, while with no variation in capital receipts and one per cent decrease in capital expenditure the surplus increases by that amount.

One per cent increase in capital receipts without any variation in capital expenditure increases the surplus by Rs. 206 crores, as compared to the budget estimate, and the surplus is reduced by the same amount if there is one per cent decrease in capital receipts without any change in the capital expenditure.

There is increase of Rs. 401 crores in surplus, as compared to the budget estimate, if there is one per cent increase in capital receipt and one per cent decrease in capital expenditure and the surplus is reduced by the same amount if there is one per cent decrease in capital receipts and one per cent increase in capital expenditure .

39. In the case of overall surplus/deficit, the variations will be larger in number, as the extent of variation will be different with each kind of variation in revenue surplus/deficit discussed in paragraph 37 in combination with any of the

variations in surplus/deficit in capital account indicated in paragraph 38 .

40.1 It will be clear from paragraphs 34, 35, 36, 37 and 38 that it is difficult to lay down any limit for variation between budget estimate and actual. In the case of any excess expenditure over the amount voted (in a grant) by Parliament, post-facto approval of the Parliament in the form of excess grant is necessary under Article 115 of the Constitution of India for the excess expenditure, even if the excess is of one rupee. In the cases of savings in expenditure or variations in receipts no fresh approval of Parliament is necessary. But the Comptroller and Auditor General makes his own observations on such variations in his presentation of accounts. The reasons for which accuracy is necessary in making estimates in the budget have already been discussed earlier in paragraphs 34.1.1 and 34.1.2. It all depends on each of the large number of estimating authorities to realise the importance of ensuring accuracy in budgeting and sincerely work for fulfilment of that objective applying "the same prudence which an ordinary individual will apply in planning his own expenditure keeping in view his resource position" vide paragraph 34.1.2.

40.2 From the details given earlier it would appear that the variations in the case of Central Government in most of the financial years under review were quite high both in respect of receipts and expenditure. It may be that in some years the variations resulting in lesser deficit or more surplus were due to post budget economy measures adopted in the course of the year or greater efforts to raise additional resources. However, the need for economy measures and mobilising additional resources being already known to Government for many years now, these aspects should have been taken into account while framing the estimates, so that there was least possible variation between the budget estimate and actuals.

40.3 Although revenue deficit actually occurred in 1979-80 for the first time and have been continuing since then the budget estimates have been showing revenue deficit since 1977-78. On the other hand, receipts and expenditure on capital account have been showing surplus since 1987-88. As has already been discussed in paragraph 28, it is of utmost importance for us to put a stop to the revenue deficit which has been persisting since 1979-80. There is also no reason for satisfaction in having a surplus on capital account. Where does such surplus on capital account go? The so called surplus on capital account goes to finance the revenue deficit, i.e. revenue expenditure in excess of revenue receipts. It can never be a prudent financial policy to use surplus on capital account, which in fact means borrowed funds at high interest rates and meant for investment in productive and durable assets or liquidating recurring liabilities, for expenditure on revenue account when money vanishes without creating any productive asset or reducing recurring liabilities .

PART VI – ECONOMIC AND FUNCTIONAL CLASSIFICATION OF CENTRAL GOVERNMENT BUDGET

Chapters

I

GENERAL

41.1.1 Government budgets follow the prescribed accounting classifications. The actual figures of receipts and expenditure (as against the estimated figures in the budget) are the figures of annual accounts of each financial year. These figures appearing in accounts have their utility in enabling the Government to plan its future mobilisation of resources and their application. But it is not possible to determine from these accounts figures the effects of the budget in the economy of the country. Economists have their own criteria for classifying the actual figures of expenditure (application of resources) for various purposes and determining the effect or usefulness of the same in economic terms.

41.1.2 Similarly, although Government accounting system provides for sectoral and functional classification of the figures of expenditure (application of resources) for various purposes, the figures relating to each sector and function are scattered in the different parts of annual accounts such as revenue expenditure and capital expenditure. Again, the figures of expenditure under revenue expenditure and capital expenditure are divided into 'Plan' expenditure and 'non Plan' expenditure. As such, the figures of expenditure appearing in the annual accounts of a financial year do not show in one place what is the total expenditure under a particular function or even under a sector covering several functions. The figures in accounts (and, therefore, budget) are not readily useful for the economists. These have to be re-grouped on the basis of economic and functional criteria for their study; this is economic and functional classification of Government budgetary transactions.

41.2 Since 1967-68, the Government of India has been bringing out an economic and functional classification of the budgetary transactions for each financial year. The purpose of such economic and functional classification of budgetary transactions of the Government of India has been stated in the Reserve Bank of India's Report on Currency and Finance, 1988-89 (page 258- Volume I) as for the "proper appreciation and understanding of the economic impact of its transactions with a view to making the budget a more useful tool for economic analysis". In making economic and functional classification of its budgetary transactions, Government of India adopts the methodology and concepts used in the National Accounting System.

II

ECONOMIC CLASSIFICATION

A. Resources

42.1 In the economic classification of the budgetary transactions of the Central Government, its total receipts are classified under the following heads:

(i) Current receipts
(Tax and non-tax receipts)

(ii) Capital transfers
(Cash grants from foreign countries and international organisations and also aid material and equipment).

(iii) Internal resources of Departmental Undertakings (Provisions for depreciation and retained profits of the departmental commercial undertakings).

(iv) Recovery of loan.

The difference between the total receipts thus worked out and the total expenditure is therefore shown as financed by (expenditure being in excess of receipts), (i) net external borrowings and (ii) net domestic borrowings (which include net market loans, net receipts under small savings schemes, net receipts under provident funds, net special deposits of non-Government provident funds, special borrowings from the Reserve Bank of India against compulsory deposits, net miscellaneous capital receipts, net special securities and net increase/decrease in holding of Treasury Bills by parties other than the Reserve Bank of India).

The balance of the excess expenditure is shown as budgetary deficit.

42.2 The economic classification of the resources as per budget of 1997-98 has been shown as below in a statement called "Sources and Uses of Funds – Central Government" on page 185 of the volume II of Reserve Bank of India's Report on Currency and Finance, 1997-98.

		1997-98 *(Rs. in Crores)*
1.	Current receipts (excluding post budget tax concessions)	149311
2.	Capital Transfers	1100
3.	Internal Resources of Departmental Undertakings	10668
4.	Recovery of Loans	8469
5.	Disinvestment in shares	4800
	Total Receipts (1 to 5)	174348
	Excess of Total Expenditure (Rs. 2,43,195 crores) over Total Receipts Financed by	68847
	1. Net Domestic Borrowings	66412
	2. Net External Borrowings	2435

B. Application of Resources

43.1.1 In the economic classification of budgetary transactions of the Central Government, its total expenditure is broadly divided into (i) its own final outlays and (ii) financial resources provided to the rest of the economy comprising states and Union Territories, non-departmental Commercial Undertakings, local authorities and foreign Governments.

43.1.2 The final outlays of the Central Government are divided into consumption expenditure and expenditure on gross capital formation.

43.1.3 The financial resources provided to the rest of the economy include financial investments and loans to the rest of the economy and are divided into (i) financial resources provided for capital formation and (ii) the financial resources provided for purposes other than capital formation. The expression "rest of the economy" includes State Government, Union Territories, aided institutions, etc.

43.1.4 From the details mentioned above the break-up of the expenditure for capital formation and that for purposes other than capital formation is worked out.

43.2 The economic classification of total budgetary expenditure of the Central Government for 1997-98 is shown below

	1997-98 (Rs. in Crores)
I. Total expenditure (A+B)	2,43,195
A. Final Outlays (a+b)	78,704
(a) Consumption Expenditure	56,753
(b) Gross Capital Formation	21,951
B. Financial Resources provided to the rest of the Economy(a+b)	1,64,491
(a) For capital formation	47,257
(b) For purposes other than capital formation	1,17,234
II. Total expenditure for gross capital formation	69,208
III. Total expenditure for purposes other than capital formation	1,73,987
The total expenditure for gross capital formation includes increase in inventories to the extent of Rs. 336 crores.	
The total expenditure for purposes other than capital formation includes the following (a+b):	
(a) Current expenditure (i+ii)	1,68,552
(i) Consumption expenditure	56,753
(ii) Current transfers	1,11,799
(b) Other expenditures	5,435
	1,73,987

Consumption Expenditure

44.1.1 The growth of the consumption expenditure of the Central Government over the years has been as follows:

Year	Total expenditure	Consumption expenditure	Consumption expenditure as percentage of total expenditure
1	2	3	4
1960-61	1,806	433	24
1970-71	5,577	1,669	30
1971-72	6,710	2,055	31
1972-73	7,849	2,262	29
1973-74	8,131	2,313	28
1974-75	9,785	2,867	29
1975-76	12,037	3,449	29

(Contd.)

1	2	3	4
1976-77	13,150	3,606	27
1977-78	14,986	3,678	25
1978-79	17,717	3,976	22
1979-80	18,504	4,502	24
1980-81	22,495	5,174	23
1981-82	25,401	6,096	24
1982-83	30,494	7,057	23
1983-84	35,988	8,130	23
1984-85	43,879	9,428	22
1985-86	53,112	11,210	21
1986-87	64,023	14,665	23
1987-88	70,305	16,551	24
1988-89	80,627	18,763	23
1989-90	94,246	20,784	22
1990-91	1,04,973	23,359	21
1991-92	1,12,731	24,466	22
1992-93	1,25,927	26,865	21
1993-94	1,45,788	31,815	22
1994-95	1,66,998	34,878	21
1995-96	1,85,233	41,881	23
1996-97 (RE)	2,13,931	47,175	22
1997-98 (BE)	2,43,195	56,753	23

44.1.2 The figures in the above table shows that as the total expenditure of the Central Government has increased from Rs. 1806 crores in 1960-61 to Rs. 94246 in 1989-90, the consumption expenditure has increased more or less at the same pace from Rs. 433 crores in 1960-61 to Rs. 20,784 crores in 1989-90. Thereafter, total expenditure of the Central Government increased from Rs. 1,04,973 crores in 1990-91 to Rs. 2,43,195 crores in 1997-98 (BE). The consumption expenditure increased from Rs. 23,359 crores in 1990-91 to Rs. 56,753 crores in 1997-98 (B.E). That is why there has not been very wide variation in consumption expenditure as a percentage of total expenditure. Although, by 1970-71, the consumption expenditure as a percentage of total expenditure rose to 30 per cent and further rose to 31 per cent in 1971-72 as compared to 24 per cent in 1960-61, the same gradually came down to 25 per cent (in 1985-86) and 24 per cent (1979-80, 1981-82 and 1987-88), and varied between 21 and 28 per cent thereafter. Thus, if measured as percentage of total expenditure, consumption expenditure has not increased disproportionately. But this does not give a correct picture because out of the total expenditure of the Central Government 60 to 70 per cent goes as transfer payment and financial investment to the rest of the economy vide paragraph 46.1.1. It would, therefore, be more appropriate to measure consumption expenditure of the Central Government as percentage of its final outlay.

44.1.3 If the consumption expenditure of the Central Government is measured as percentage of its own final outlays, the following position emerges:

Year	Final Outlays of the Central Government	Consumption expenditure	Consumption expenditure as percent of final outlays of the Central Government
1	2	3	4
1960-61	741	433	58
1970-71	2189	1669	76
1971-72	2652	2055	77
1972-73	2939	2262	77
1973-74	3095	2313	75
1974-75	4094	2867	70
1975-76	4654	3449	73
1976-77	4718	3606	76
1977-78	4786	3678	77
1978-79	5276	3976	75
1979-80	6030	4502	75
1980-81	7082	5174	73
1981-82	8648	6096	70
1982-83	9941	7057	71
1983-84	11486	8130	71
1984-85	13552	9428	70
1985-86	15768	11210	71
1986-87	20570	14665	71

(Contd.)

1	2	3	4
1987-88	22512	16551	74
1988-89	25819	18763	73
1989-90	28920	20784	73
1990-91	30961	22359	72
1991-92	33725	24466	73
1992-93	38739	26865	69
1993-94	44580	31815	71
1994-95	49206	34878	71
1995-96	58566	41881	72
1996-97 (RE)	65997	47175	71
1997-98 (BE)	78704	56753	72

44.1.4 It will be noticed from the above that consumption expenditure of the Central Government rose to 76 per cent of its final outlays in 1970-71 as against 58 per cent in 1960-61. This rose to 77 per cent in 1971-72 and remained so in 1972-73. There was slight decline in 1973-74 to 75 per cent followed by a sharp decline to 70 per cent in 1974-75. Between 1975-76 and 1979-80, the share of consumption expenditure to the final outlays of the Central Government remained between 73 and 77 per cent. In the next decade starting 1980-81, the share of consumption expenditure to final outlays of the Central Government was 70 per cent in 1981-82 and 1984-85, 71 per cent in 1982-83, 1983-84, 1985-86, 1986-87, 1993-94 and 1994-95, 72 per cent in 1988-89, 1990-91, 1995-96 and 1997-98, 73 per cent in 1980-81 and 1991-92 and 74 per cent in 1987-88. Only in 1992-93 it was 69 per cent.

44.1.5 Thus it will be seen that most of the final outlays of the Central Government in each financial year goes for consumption expenditure.

44.2 The main share in consumption expenditure was that of defence as will be evident from the following table:

However, in the recent years the share of expenditure on defence has gradually come down from 71 per cent of consumption expenditure in 1987-88 to 62 per cent in 1997-98 (B.E), except for slight rises in 1990-91 and 1993-94.

(Rupees in Crores)

Year	Consumption expenditure	Expenditure on Defence	Expenditure on Defence as percentage of Consumption expenditure
1	2	3	4
1980-81	5174	3571	69
1981-82	6096	4327	71
1982-83	7057	5018	71
1983-84	8130	5823	72
1984-85	9428	6647	71
1985-86	11210	7962	71
1986-87	14665	10439	71
1987-88	16551	11875	72
1988-89	18763	13237	71
1989-90	20784	14381(RE)	69
1990-91	22359	15619 (BE)	70
1991-92	24466	16251	66
1992-93	26865	17402	65
1993-94	31815	21608	68
1994-95	34878	22891	66
1995-96	41881	26257	63
1996-97 (RE)	47175	29384	62
1997-98 (BE)	56753	35434	62

Capital Formation

45.1.1 The table in paragraph 44.1.3 shows how much of the final outlays of the Central Government is utilised for consumption expenditure. The balance of the final outlays of the Central Government is utilised for its own gross capital formation, in other words, this is the direct investment of the Central Government for its own gross capital formation.

45.1.2 Direct investment of the Central Government for its own gross capital formation is in the shape of (i) construction works, (ii) machinery and equipment, and (iii) increase in works stores. But this investment also includes expenditure on renewals and replacement of existing assets. When the expenditure on such renewals and replacements of existing assets is deducted from the direct investment of the Central Government for its own gross capital formation, the net direct investment of the Central Government for its capital formation is known. For example, according to the figures of budget estimate for 1997-98, the direct investment of the Central Government for gross capital formation was Rs. 21,951 crores. The expenditure on renewals and replacements according to the budget of that year was Rs. 3911 crores. The direct investment of the Central Government for net capital formation was thus Rs. 18,040 crores as per details below:

1997-98	(Budget estimate)	Rs. Crores
1.	Construction works	8311
2.	Machinery & Equipment	9739
3.	Increase in works stores	-10
		18040

45.2.1 The following table shows how much of the final outlays of the Central Government is utilised for capital formation and what proportion the same bears to the total expenditure and the final outlays of the Central Government.

Year	Total expenditure of the Central Govt.	Total final outlays of Central Govt. (excl. funds provided to the rest of the economy)	Total expenditure on Capital formation out of the final out lays of the Central Govt.	Expenditure on Capital formation out of the final outlays of the Central Govt. as a percentage of	
				Total Expenditure	Total final outlays
1	2	3	4	5	6
1960-61	1806	741	308	17	42
1970-71	5577	2189	520	9	24
1971-72	6710	2652	597	9	23
1972-73	7849	2939	677	9	23

(Contd.)

1	2	3	4	5	6
1973-74	8131	3095	782	10	25
1974-75	9785	4094	1227	13	30
1975-76	12037	4654	1205	10	27
1976-77	13150	4718	1112	9	24
1977-78	14986	4786	1108	7	23
1978-79	17717	5276	1300	8	25
1979-80	18504	6030	1528	8	25
1980-81	22495	7082	1908	8	27
1981-82	25401	8648	2552	10	30
1982-83	30494	9941	2884	10	29
1983-84	36988	11486	3356	10	29
1984-85	43879	13552	4124	9	30
1985-86	53112	15768	4558	9	29
1986-87	64023	20570	5905	9	29
1987-88	70305	22512	5961	8	26
1988-89	80627	25819	7056	9	27
1989-90	94246	28920	8136	9	28
1990-91	104973	30961	8601	8	28
1991-92	112731	33725	9259	8	27
1992-93	125927	38739	11875	9	30
1993-94	145788	44580	12765	9	29
1994-95	166998	49206	14328	9	29
1995-96	185233	58566	16685	9	28
1996-97 (RE)	213931	65997	18822	9	29
1997-98 (BE)	243195	78704	21951	9	28

45.2.2 The table above shows that as a proportion of the total expenditure of the Central Government, expenditure on its own capital formation was 17 per cent in 1960-61. This went down to 9 per cent in 1970-71 and remained at that till 1972-73. In 1973-74, it rose to 10 per cent and in the following year (1974-75) it rose further to 13 per cent. Thereafter, the proportion of the expenditure on its own capital formation to the total expenditure of the Central Government varied between 8 and 10 per cent except in 1977-78, when it had declined to 7 per cent.

45.2.3 Because of the ever increasing consumption expenditure of the Central Government, proportion of its investment for gross capital formation to the total final outlays of the Central Government declined to 24 per cent by 1970-71 as compared to 42 per cent in a decade earlier in 1960-61. Thereafter, this proportion has hovered around 23 per cent and 30 per cent till 1997-98 (BE).

45.3.1 Besides the direct investment of the Central Government for capital formation, financial resources provided to the rest of the economy are also invested for capital formation. If the gross capital formation out of such resources transferred to the rest of the economy is added to the gross capital formation by the Central Government, we get the figure of the total investment for gross capital formation out of the total expenditure of the Central Government. The following table shows the total investment for gross capital formation as compared to the total expenditure of the Central Government:

(In crores of Rupees)

Year	Total expenditure of Central Govt.	Gross capital formation from final outlays of Central Govt.	Gross capital formation from financial resources provided to the rest of the economy	Total Investment for gross capital formation	Total gross capital formation as percentage to total expenditure of Central Govt.
1	2	3	4	5	6
1960-61	1806	308	554	862	48
1970-71	5577	520	1285	1805	32
1971-72	6710	597	1605	2202	33
1972-73	7849	677	1950	2627	24
1973-74	8131	782	1882	2664	33
1974-75	9785	1227	2450	3677	38
1975-76	12037	1205	3458	4663	39
1976-77	13150	1112	3879	4991	38
1977-78	14986	1108	4580	5688	38
1978-79	17717	1300	5612	6912	39
1979-80	18504	1528	5701	7229	39
1980-81	22495	1908	7104	9012	40
1981-82	25401	2552	8247	10799	42

(Contd.)

1	2	3	4	5	6
1982-83	30494	2884	9520	12404	40
1983-84	35988	3356	11346	14702	41
1984-85	43879	4124	13427	17551	40
1985-86	53112	4558	16919	21477	41
1986-87	64023	5905	18415	24320	38
1987-88	70305	5961	19809	25770	36
1988-89	80627	7056	21921	28977	36
1989-90	84246	8136	24876	33012	35
1990-91	104973	8601	26456	35057	33
1991-92	112731	9259	25906	35165	31
1992-93	125927	11875	25774	37649	30
1993-94	145788	12765	32286	45051	31
1994-95	166998	14328	39872	54200	32
1995-96	185233	16685	38591	55276	30
1996-97 (RE)	213931	18822	43190	62012	29
1997-98 (BE)	243195	21951	47257	69208	28

45.3.2 It will appear from the above table that in 1960-61, 48 per cent of the total expenditure of the Central Government was for gross capital formation. This went down to 32 per cent in 1970-71 and thereafter varied between 33 per cent and 34 per cent during 1971-72 and 1973-74. Between 1974-75 and 1986-87, total investment for capital formation varied from 38 per cent to 42 per cent of the total expenditure of the Central Government. This went down to 36 per cent in 1987-88 and remained the same in 1988-89. In 1989-90 the total investment for gross capital formation was 35 per cent of the total expenditure of the Central Government; it went down to 33 per cent in 1990-91 and thereafter varied between 28 per cent and 32 per cent during 1991-92 to 1997-98 (B.E.).

Financial Resources Provided to the Rest of the Economy

46.1.1 Financial resources provided to the rest of the economy are in the shape of transfer payment to the rest of the economy and financial investment and loans to the rest of the economy. As mentioned in paragraph 43.1.3, the financial resources provided to the rest of the economy are for capital formation (paragraphs 45.3.1 and 45.3.2) and for purposes other than capital formation.

The figures of financial resources provided to the rest of the economy are shown in the following table:

Year	Total expenditure of the Central Government	Financial resources provided to the rest of the economy	Financial resources provided to the rest of the economy as percentage of the total expenditure of the Central Govt.
	(Rupees in Crores)		
1960-61	1806	1065	59
1970-71	5577	3388	61
1971-72	6710	4058	60
1972-73	7849	4910	62
1973-74	8131	5036	62
1974-75	9785	5691	58
1975-76	12037	7383	61
1976-77	13150	8432	64
1977-78	14986	10200	68
1978-79	17717	12441	70
1979-80	18504	12774	68
1980-81	22495	15413	69
1981-82	25401	16753	66
1982-83	30494	20553	67
1983-84	35988	24502	68
1984-85	43879	30327	69
1985-86	53112	37344	70
1986-87	64023	43453	68
1987-88	70305	47793	68
1988-89	80627	54808	68
1989-90	94246	65326	69
1990-91	104973	74012	70
1991-92	112731	79006	70
1992-93	125927	87188	69
1993-94	145788	101208	69
1994-95	166998	117792	70
1995-96	185233	126667	68
1996-97 (RE)	213931	147934	69
1997-98 (BE)	243195	164491	67

46.1.2 The preceding table shows that the financial resources provided to the rest of the economy accounted for 59 per cent of the total expenditure of the Central Government in 1960-61. After a decade, this rose to only 61 per cent in 1970-71, declined to 60 per cent in 1971-72, remained at 62 per cent in 1972-73 and 1973-74, declined to 58 per cent in 1974-75 (at a level lower than that of 1960-61) and increased again to 61 per cent in 1975-76. The proportion of financial resources provided to the rest of the economy further increased to 64 per cent in 1976-77, 68 per cent in 1977-78 and 70 per cent in 1978-79. Between 1979-80 and 1997-98 (BE), the proportion of financial resources provided to the rest of the economy to the total expenditure of the Central Government varied between 66 per cent and 70 per cent.

Savings of the Central Government

47.1.1 In the Economic and Functional Classification of the Central Government budget the savings are worked out in the following manner:

		1997-98 (Budget Estimate)
1.	Revenue Receipts of the Government Administration (i & ii)	149310
	(i) Tax Revenue	113394
	(ii) Non-Tax Revenue	35916
2.	Current Expenditure	168551
3.	Savings of the Government Administration (1-2)	-19241
4.	Depreciation Provision and Retained Profits of the Departmental Commercial Undertakings (i+ii)	10668
	(i) Depreciation Provision	3992
	(ii) Retained Profits	6676
5.	Gross Savings of the Central Government (3+4)	-8573
6.	Expenditure on Renewals and Replacements	3911
7.	Net Savings (5+6)	12484
8.	Net Direct Investments	18040
9.	Excess (+) or shortfall (-) of Net Savings (7-8)	-30524

47.1.2 The revenue receipts of the Government Administration shown in the above table are the current receipts (excluding post budget tax concessions) shown in the statement "Sources and Uses of Funds – Central Government" mentioned in paragraph 42.2.

47.1.3 The current expenditure includes consumption expenditure and current transfer as shown in paragraph 42.2.

47.1.4 The depreciation provision and retained profits of the departmental commercial undertakings shown above is the internal resources of departmental undertakings shown in paragraph 42.2.

47.1.5 The expenditure on renewals and replacements of existing assets amounting to Rs. 3911 crores in 1997-98 (budget estimate) has been mentioned in paragraph 45.1.2. The figures of net direct investments shown in the preceding statement is the same as that of the direct investment of the Central Government for net capital formation shown in paragraph 45.1.2.

47.2 The net savings and the excess or shortfall of net savings i.e. net savings minus net direct investment were as follows during the period from 1985-86 to 1997-98 (BE).

(Rupees in Crores)

Year	Net Savings	Net Direct Investments	Excess (+) or shortfall (-) of Net Savings
1985-86	-2587	3412	-5999
1986-87	-4191	4566	-8757
1987-88	-5665	4589	-10254
1988-89	-7434	5343	-12777
1989-90	-7730	6353	-14083
1990-91	-8438	6916	-15354
1991-92	-10243	6818	-17061
1992-93	-11379	8897	-20276
1993-94	-23178	9922	-33100
1994-95	-16753	11458	-28211
1995-96	-13126	13394	-26250
1996-97 (RE)	-11058	15143	-26201
1997-98 (BE)	-12484	18040	-30524

Income Generation of the Budgetary Operations of the Central Government

48.1 The economic and functional classification of the Central Government Budget also contains a statement showing income generation of the budgetary operations of the Central Government. The total income generation of the budgetary operations of the Central Government for the years 1993-94 to 1997-98 (BE) has been worked out as follows:

(Rs. in crores)

	1993-94	1994-95	1995-96	1996-97 (RE)	1997-98 (BE)
1. Wages and Salaries paid by Govt. Administration	13357	14694	17036	19006	29344
2. Net output of departmental commercial undertakings (a+b+c)	16073	19977	21961	25121	28206
(a) Wages and salaries (including wages and salaries component of repairs and maintenance operations)	9594	10474	11819	13451	16767
(b) Interest	2410	2608	2678	3361	3940
(c) Profits (transferred to administration and retained plus excess of depreciation provision over renewals and replacements)	4069	6895	7464	8309	7500
3. Wages and Salaries components of Government outlays on construction	1719	2105	2175	2330	2770
Total (1+2+3)	31149	36578	41172	47057	60320

48.2 It will appear from the above table that the wages and salaries paid by Government administration in 1994-95 increased by 8.5 per cent as compared to 1993-94. In 1995-

96, the increase was 17.5 per cent as compared to 1994-95. The revised estimate for 1996-97 showed an increase of 11.5 per cent in the wages and salaries paid by Government administration as compared to 1995-96, while the increase in budget for the year 1997-98 was 54.4 per cent over 1996-97 (RE). The increase in 1997-98 (BE) as compared to 1993-94 was over 119.7 per cent.

48.3 The wages and salaries in departmental commercial undertakings increased in 1994-95 by 19.2 per cent as compared to 1993-94. The increase in 1995-96 as compared to 1994-95 was 12.8 per cent. The revised estimate for 1996-97 showed an increase of 3.8 per cent over 1995-96. The budget for 1997-98 showed an increase of 18.6 per cent as compared to 1996-97 (RE). The increase in the wages and salaries in departmental commercial undertakings in the budget estimate for 1997-98 was 74.8 per cent as compared to 1993-94.

48.4 The profits of departmental undertakings in 1994-95 were 69.4 per cent more than that in 1993-94. In 1995-96, these profits increased by 8.3 per cent over that in 1994-95. The profits in 1996-97 (RE) were 11.3 per cent more than the same in 1995-96. The profits in 1997-98 (BE) were 9.7 per cent less than the profits 1996-97 (RE). As compared to 1993-94, the profits in 1997-98 (BE) were 84.3 per cent more.

48.5 The wages and salaries components of Government outlays on construction showed an increase of 22.4 per cent in 1994-95 as compared to 1993-94. The increase in 1995-96 was 3.3 per cent as compared to 1994-95. The revised estimates of 1996-97 showed an increase of 7.1 per cent over 1995-96, while according to the budget estimates for 1997-98 the increase over the revised estimates of 1996-97 was 18.8 per cent.

48.6 In 1994-95, interest increased by 8.2 per cent as compared to 1993-94. Interest in 1995-96 was 2.7 per cent more than 1994-95. The revised estimate of 1996-97 for interest was 25.5 per cent more than 1995-96. Interest in 1997-98 (BE), was 17.2 per cent more than 1996-97 (RE). In 1997-98 (BE), interest was 63.5 per cent more than that in 1993-94.

48.7 The total income generations of the budgetary operations of the Central Government in 1994-95 increased by 17.4 per cent as compared to 1993-94. The increase in 1995-96 as compared to 1994-95 was 12.6 per cent. The revised estimates for 1996-97 showed an increase of 14.3 per cent over 1995-96 and the budget estimates for 1997-98 showed an increase of 28.2 per cent as compared to the revised estimates for 1996-97.

III

FUNCTIONAL CLASSIFICATION

49. Accounting classification of Government expenditure provides for classification by functions under different sectors such as social services, economic services, general services, etc. Expenditure on education, art and culture, health, scientific services, social services, etc. which are treated as functions, fall under social services. Economic Services include expenditure on agriculture, industry, transport and communications, energy, etc. General Services include expenditure on various organs of administration, fiscal services, interest payment and debt servicing, administrative services etc. However, as mentioned in para 41.1.2 the annual accounts of Government do not show in one place the figures of expenditure under any function or sector.

50.1 Since the country has been making efforts for planned development, it is important to know in the first instance what has been the expenditure on development, the extent of non-development expenditure and the proportion of development and non-development expenditure to the total expenditure of the Central Government; the following table gives these details for the years 1976-77 to 1989-90 (BE).

Year	Total expenditure of the Central Govt. (Rs. Cr.)	Development expenditure of the Central Govt. (Rs. Cr.)	Development expenditure as per cent of total expenditure (Rs. Cr.)	Non-development expenditure of the Central Govt. (Rs. Cr.)	Non-development expenditure as per cent of total expenditure
1	2	3	4	5	6
1976-77	13150	7174	55	5976	45
1977-78	14986	8438	56	6548	44
1978-79	17717	10377	59	7340	41

(Contd.)

1	2	3	4	5	6
1979-80	18504	11112	60	7392	40
1980-81	22495	–	–	–	–
1981-82	25401	15148	60	10253	40
1982-83	30494	18095	59	12399	41
1983-84	35988	21084	59	14904	41
1984-85	43879	26276	60	17603	40
1985-86	53112	30852	58	22260	42
1986-87	64023	35872	56	28151	44
1987-88	70305	37968	54	32336	46
1988-89(RE)	82135	45017	55	37118	45
1989-90(BE)	88506	47576	54	40930	46

50.2 The first half of the nineteen seventies was a difficult period for the economy of the country. The Economic Survey for 1974-75 described that year to be by all accounts "a year of unprecedented economic strains in the history of the independent India". In that year, the proportion of development expenditure was 51 per cent of the total expenditure of the Central Government. Thereafter, this proportion rose to 60 per cent by 1979-80 and remained between 59 per cent and 60 per cent till 1984-85. The proportion of development expenditure to the total expenditure of the Central Government has shown a declining trend after that. In 1987-88, it reached 54 per cent and although the revised estimate for 1988-89 showed slight rise to 55 per cent, the budget estimates for 1989-90 showed the proportion of development expenditure as 54 per cent. This trend needs to be reversed.

50.3 The details of development expenditure, non-development expenditure and their proportion as per cent of total expenditure from 1991-92 onwards are given below:

Year	Total expenditure of Central Govt. (Rs. Cr.)	Development expenditure of the Central Govt. (Rs. Cr.)	Development expenditure as per cent of Central Government	Non-development expenditure of the Central Govt. (Rs. Cr.)	Non-development expenditure as per cent of total expenditure
1	2	3	4	5	6
1991-92	112731	51461	46	61270	54
1992-93	125927	61040	48	64887	52

(Contd.)

1	2	3	4	5	6
1993-94	145788	71064	49	74724	51
1994-95	166998	70021	42	96977	58
1995-96	185233	73818	40	111415	60
1996-97 (RE)	213931	85470	40	128461	60
1997-98 (BE)	243195	95155	39	148040	61

50.4 It will appear from the above table that the share of development expenditure came down sharply to 46 per cent in 1991-92 from 54 per cent in 1989-90 (B.E.). Thereafter, it increased to 48 per cent in 1992-93 and 49 per cent in 1993-94. But it fell sharply to 42 per cent in 1994-95 and thereafter slided down further to 40 per cent in 1995-96 and 1996-97 (R.E.) and to 39 per cent in 1997-98 (B.E.). Thus it will be seen that the share of development expenditure which rose to 60 per cent of total expenditure (in 1979-80, 1981-82 and 1984-85) has slided down to 39 per cent in 1997-98 (B.E.). This trend needs to be reversed.

51.1 In functional classification of its expenditure made by the Government of India, the non-developmental expenditure is shown under (i) General Services and (ii) Unallocable. The development expenditure is classified under (i) Social Services and (ii) Economic services. The details of expenditure of Central Government under social services and economic services and their proportion to the total development expenditure during the period from 1976-77 to 1989-90 (B.E.) are shown in the statement below:

Year	Total development expenditure of the Central Govt. (Rs. Cr.)	Expenditure on social services (Rs. Cr.)	Expenditure on social services as percentage of total development expenditure	Expenditure on economic services (Rs. Cr.)	Expenditure on economic services as percentage of total development expenditure
1	2	3	4	5	6
1976-77	7174	900	13	6274	87
1977-78	8438	970	12	7468	88
1978-79	10377	1198	12	9179	88

(Contd.)

1	2	3	4	5	6
1979-80	11112	1244	11	9868	89
1980-81	–	–	–	–	–
1981-82	15148	1545	10	13603	90
1982-83	18095	2135	12	15960	88
1983-84	21084	2557	12	18527	88
1984-85	26276	3162	12	23114	88
1985-86	30852	3882	13	26970	87
1986-87	35872	5097	14	30775	86
1987-88	37968	7140	19	30828	81
1988-89(RE)	45017	7421	16	37596	84
1989-90(BE)	47576	7503	16	40073	84

51.2 It will appear from the preceding statement that till 1985-86, only 10 to 13 per cent of the development expenditure was meant for social services. This rose to 14 per cent in 1986-87. In 1987-88 the share of social services was 19 per cent of the total development expenditure of the Central Government. In the revised estimate for 1988-89 and the budget estimate for 1989-90, the share of social services in the total development expenditure of the Central Government declined to 16 per cent.

51.3 The details of expenditure of Central Government under social services and economic services and their proportion to the total development expenditure from 1991-92 onwards are given below:

Year	Total development expenditure of Central Govt. (Rs. Cr.)	Expenditure on social services (Rs. Cr.)	Expenditure on social services as percentage of total development expenditure	Expenditure on economic services (Rs. Cr.)	Expenditure on economic services as percentage of development expenditure
1	2	3	4	5	6
1991-92	51461	10156	20	41305	80
1992-93	61040	11510	19	49530	81
1993-94	71064	13925	20	57139	80
1994-95	70021	16460	24	53561	76
1995-96	73818	18976	26	54842	74

(Contd.)

1	2	3	4	5	6
1996-97 (RE)	85470	20006	23	65464	77
1997-98 (BE)	95155	24418	26	70737	74

51.4 It will appear from the above table that the share of social services to total development expenditure which was 16 per cent in 1989-90 (B.E.) has risen gradually to 26 per cent in 1995-96 and 1997-98 (B.E.).

51.5 The share of economic services to the total development expenditure rose to 90 per cent in 1981-82 and has remained 80 per cent or above in most of the years under review. But a declining trend started in 1994-95 (76 per cent), which came down to 74 per cent in 1995-96. It rose to 77 per cent in 1996-97 (R.E.), but came down to 74 per cent again in 1997-98 (B.E.). While larger outlay for economic services is necessary for economic development of a developing country like India, the development of human resources directly by promoting education, art and culture and indirectly by promoting health care and social upliftment of under privileged, is also necessary for balanced development of a country. It is true that most of the social services sector falls in the domain of states. Nevertheless, it needs serious reconsideration whether, in view of the need for balanced development of the country, increased emphasis should be given for human resources development by augmenting the provision of funds for social services, particularly in view of the fact that about 70 per cent of the total expenditure of the Central Government is for providing financial resources to the rest of the economy, which includes provision for social services sector also. It is needless to emphasise that the fruits of development cannot be sustained unless the human resources are also developed side by side.

52.1 A statement showing economic-cum-functional classification of the total expenditure of the Central Government is also prepared for each financial year.

52.2 The following table shows the economic-cum-functional classification of the total expenditure of the Central Government for the years 1987-88, 1988-89 (R.E.) and 1989-90 (B.E.).

(Rupees in Crores)

	1987-88 (Account)		1988-89 (Revised Estimate)		1989-90 (Budget Estimate)	
	Amount	Per cent change over previous year	Amount	Per cent change over previous year	Amount	Per cent change over previous year
1	2	3	4	5	6	7
I. Final outlays (A+B+C)	22511 (5961)	+9.4 (+0.9)	26258 (7426)	+16.6 (+24.6)	28102 (8433)	+7.0 (+13.6)
(a) General Services and unallocable items	15120	+11.5	17031	+12.6	17896	+5.1
(b) Social and Economic Services	7391	+5.4	9227	+24.8	10206	+10.6
A. Consumption Expenditure (a+b)	16551	+12.9	18832	+13.8	19669	+4.4
(a) General Services and unallocable items	14754	+12.3	16491	+11.8	17189	+4.2
(b) Social and Economic Services	1797	+17.5	2341	+30.3	2480	+5.9
B. Gross Fixed Capital Formation (a+b)	5683	-2.3	7202	+26.7	8097	+12.4
(a) General Services and unallocable items	362	-11.1	501	+38.4	665	+32.7
(b) Social and Economic Services	5321	-1.6	6701	+25.9	7432	+10.9
C. Charges in Inventories (a+b)	277	+214.8	224	-19.1	336	+50.0
(a) General Services and unallocable items	4	-69.2	39	+875.0	42	+7.7
(b) Social and Economic Services	273	+264.0	185	-32.2	294	+58.9
II. Financial Resources provided to the rest of the Economy (a+b)	47793 (19809)	+10.0 (+7.6)	55877 (22207)	+16.9 (+12.1)	60404 (22301)	+8.1 (+0.4)

(Contd).

1	2	3	4	5	6	7
(a) General Services and unallocable items	17215	+17.9	20087	+16.7	23035	+14.7
(b) Social and Economic Services	30578	+6.0	35790	+17.0	37369	+4.4
A. States and Union Territories (a+b)	17908 (12723)	+19.3 (+17.8)	19786 (14119)	+10.5 (+11.0)	21361 (14371)	+8.0 (+1.8)
(a) General Services and unallocable items	1580	+29.0	1425	-9.8	2034	+42.7
(b) Social and Economic Services	16328	+18.4	18361	+12.5	19327	+5.3
B. Non-departmental Undertakings & Others (a+b)	29885 (7086)	+5.1 (-6.9)	36091 (8088)	20.8 (+14.1)	39043 (7930)	+8.2 (-2.0)
(a) General Services and unallocable items	15635	+16.9	18662	+19.4	21001	+12.5
(b) Social and Economic Services	14250	-5.4	17429	+22.3	18042	+3.5
III. Total Expenditure (I&II)	70304 (25770)	+9.8 (+6.0)	82135 (29633)	+16.8 (+15.0)	88506 (30734)	+7.8 (+3.7)
(a) General Services and unallocable items	32335	+14.9	37118	+14.8	40931	+10.3
(b) Social and Economic Services	37969	+5.8	45017	+18.6	47575	+5.7

Note: Figures in brackets represent expenditure on Gross Capital Formation.
Source: Report on Currency and Finance of Reserve Bank of India.

52.2 The expenditure on general services and unallocable items had increased in 1985-86 over 1984-85 by 26.5 per cent. This percentage of increase was maintained in 1986-87 as compared to 1985-86. The increase in 1987-88 as compared to 1986-87 declined to 14.9 per cent. In the revised estimate for 1988-89, the increase was slightly less at 14.8 per cent as compared to 1987-88. In the budget estimate for 1989-90, the increase in general services and unallocable items as compared to the revised estimate of 1988-89 declined to 10.3 per cent.

52.3 On the other hand, the increase in expenditure on social and economic services in 1985-86 was 17.4 per cent as compared to 1984-85. The increase in 1986-87 as compared to 1985-86, was less at 16.3 per cent. The rate of increase in 1987-88 sharply declined to 5.8 per cent as compared to 1986-87. However, in the revised estimate for 1988-89 the increase was 18.6 per cent as compared to 1987-88; in this year the rate of increase in expenditure on social and economic services surpassed the rate of increase of expenditure on general services, etc. But in the budget estimate for 1989-90, the rate of increase for social and economic services declined to 5.7 per cent as compared to the revised estimate for 1988-89.

52.4 Thus, it will be seen that except for 1988-89 (revised estimate) the rate of increase of expenditure on general services, etc. exceeded the rate of increase in social and economic services. This aspect needs serious consideration.

52.5 A table showing the economic-cum-functional classification of the total expenditure of the Central Government for the years 1994-95 to 1997-98 (BE) is given below:

Economic-cum-functional classification of the total expenditure of Government of India

(Rupees in Crores)

Item	1995-96 (Accounts)		1996-97 (Revised Estimates)		1997-98 (Budget Estimates)	
	Amount	Percentage change over the previous year	Amount	Percentage change over the previous year	Amount	Percentage change over the previous year
1	2	3	4	5	6	7
I. Final outlays (A+B+C)	58566 (16685)	+19.0 (+16.5)	65997 (18822)	+12.7 (+12.8)	78704 (21951)	+19.3 (+16.6)
(a) General Services and unallocable items	35561	+15.3	40735	+14.5	51772	+27.1
(b) Social and Economic Services	23005	+25.3	25262	+9.8	26932	+6.6

(Contd.)

1	2	3	4	5	6	7
A. Consumption Expenditure (a+b)	41881	+20.1	47175	+12.6	56753	+20.3
(a) General Services and unallocable items	34865	+15.8	39504	+13.3	50315	+27.4
(b) Social and Economic Services	7016	+47.2	7671	+9.3	6438	-16.1
B. Gross Fixed Capital Formation (a+b)	16858	+13.9	18902	+12.1	21961	+16.2
(a) General Services and unallocable items	931	+15.5	1151	+23.6	1329	+15.5
(b) Social and Economic Services	15927	+13.8	17751	+11.5	20632	+16.2
C. Changes in Inventories (a+b)	-173	-136.3	-80	-53.8	-10	-87.5
(a) General Services and unallocable items	35	-152.2	80	+128.6	128	+60.0
(b) Social and Economic Services	-208	-49.1	-160	-23.1	-138	-13.8
II. Financial Resources provided to the rest of the Economy (A+B)	126667 (38591)	+7.5 (-3.2)	147934 (43190)	+16.8 (+11.9)	164491 (47257)	+11.2 (+9.4)
(a) General Services and unallocable items	75585	+14.3	87726	+16.1	96265	+9.7
(b) Social and Economic Services	51082	-1.1	60208	+17.9	68226	+13.3
A. States and Union Territories (a+b)	40873 (27571)	+4.5 (+0.6)	47438 (32973)	+16.1 (+19.6)	48612 (33850)	+2.5 (+2.7)
(a) General Services and unallocable items	16303	+12.8	16838	+3.3	16143	-4.1
(b) Social and Economic Services	24570	-0.3	30600	+24.5	32469	+6.1
B. Non-departmental Undertakings & Other Parties (a+b)	85794 (11020)	+9.0 (-11.5)	100496 (10217)	+17.1 (-7.3)	115879 (13407)	+15.3 (+31.2)

(Contd.)

1	2	3	4	5	6	7
(a) General Services and unallocable items	59282	+14.7	70888	+19.6	80122	+13.0
(b) Social and Economic Services	26512	-1.9	29608	+11.7	35757	+20.8
III. Total Expenditure (I & II)	185233 (55276)	+10.9 (+2.0)	213931 (62012)	+15.5 (+12.2)	243195 (69208)	+13.7 (+11.6)
(a) General Services and unallocable items	111415	+14.9	128461	+15.3	148040	+15.2
(b) Social and Economic Services	73818	+5.4	85470	+15.8	95155	+11.3

Note: Figures in brackets represent expenditure on Gross Capital Formation.
Source: Report on Currency and Finance of the Reserve Bank of India for the year 1997-98.

52.6 It will appear from the above table that the rate of growth of expenditure on general services and unallocable items continued to be higher than that of expenditure on social and economic services except in 1996-97, when the rate of growth of the latter was slightly higher. In 1994-95, the expenditure on social and economic services was considerably lower than that in the previous year.

PART VII – EPILOGUE

I

EPILOGUE

53.1 In the earlier chapters, comparisons have been made with reference to the figures of receipts and expenditure of the Central Government. Before I conclude, it perhaps needs explaining why comparison has been restricted amongst these figures themselves, instead of comparing these figures with the figures of GDP as is usually done in the Economic Survey or in the Reports on Currency and Finance published by the Reserve Bank of India. Due to the inflationary effects, GDP for a year is no longer a constant figure. With the change in base year, for calculating GDP with reference to the price level of the base year, GDP for a year undergoes change. As a result, the proportions of the receipts and expenditure figures of a year, except for the base year, undergo change. For the same reason, the proportions of the receipts and expenditure figures to the Net National Product also undergo change as will be evident from the following figures showing the total tax revenue of Centre, States and Union Territories as per cent of net national product at current prices and at 1980-81 prices.

(Rs. in crores)

Year	Total Tax Revenue of Centre, States & Union Territories	Net National Product at current prices	Net National Product at 1980-81 prices	Total tax revenue as % of net national product at current prices	Total tax revenue as per cent of net national product at 1980-81 prices
1	2	3	4	5	6
1950-51	627	8525	40454	7.35	1.55
1955-56	768	9106	48288	8.43	1.59

(Contd.)

1	2	3	4	5	6
1960-61	1350	14160	58602	9.53	2.30
1965-66	2922	22107	65734	13.22	4.45
1970-71	4752	36362	82211	13.07	5.78
1975-76	11182	64531	95433	17.33	11.72
1980-81	19844	110484	110484	17.36	17.36
1985-86	43267	206491	139804	20.35	30.35
1986-87	49540	228708	144828	21.66	34.20
1987-88	56976	257913	149967	22.09	37.99
1988-89	65443	306822	166593	21.33	39.28

53.2 It will appear from the above table that the comparison with the figures of Net National Product at 1980-81 prices gives much more favourable percentage for the years following 1980-81 than those at current prices. On the other hand, the figures of percentages give comparatively much more unfavourable picture for the years preceding 1980-81 with reference to the higher figures of Net National Product at 1980-81 prices. The reasons for the above position are as follows:

(i) While the figures of Net National Product at 1980-81 prices have increased for the years preceding 1980-81 and have decreased for the years following 1980-81, the figures of tax revenue remain the same as these are account figures.

(ii) Collection of tax revenue was made in the years prior to 1980-81 on lower tax base at current prices.

(iii) In the post 1980-81 years, the tax base became higher at current prices because of inflationary effect.

Incidentally, in recent years economists have expressed doubt about dependability of GNP/GDP as an index of measuring growth (Development Digest, October 1971, Page 71 –Dr. Mahabub-Ul-Haq).

53.3 The figures of budget or accounts remain unaltered and, as such, comparisons have been made amongst the figures of receipts and expenditure as per budget or accounts.

54. From the earlier chapters, it will appear that the Government of India is well aware of the reasons for its fiscal imbalances,

which, in the main, are as follows:

(i) continuous unwieldy growth of consumption expenditure

(ii) inadequate return on its huge capital investments from borrowed funds including foreign loans,

(iii) narrow base of its tax structure.

55.1.1 The Government of India is also aware of the possible solutions, as discussed below, which have been mentioned in its Economic Surveys of different financial years, some of which have been quoted earlier and some others are quoted below:

(a) The important policy initiatives introduced in the budget for 1991-92 for correcting the fiscal imbalance have been mentioned in paragraph 2.6 of the Economic Survey for 1992-93 (Part II) as follows:

(i) Reduction in the fertiliser subsidy by increasing the average prices of fertilisers by 30 per cent (except for marginal and small farmers).

(ii) Abolition of cash compensatory support for exports.

(iii) Abolition of subsidy on sugar distributed through the Public Distribution System by increasing the price by 85 paise per kg. to Rs. 6.10 per kg.

(iv) Offering of up to 20 per cent of Government equity in selected public sector undertakings to mutual funds and investment institutions in the public sector. This is estimated to fetch the Government Rs. 2500 crores.

(v) A 20 per cent increase in the prices of motor spirit, domestic LPG and aviation turbine fuel for domestic use.

(vi) Adjustment of tax rates to yield an additional net revenue of Rs. 2005 crores to the Centre.

In addition, the Government had also imposed in September 1991 a five per cent cut on the expenditure provision in the budget for 1991-92 except for statutory grants to State Governments, block grants and loans for State Plan Schemes, interest payments and pension payments.

(b) In a statement made by the Finance Minister in Parliament on 16 December 1991 it was indicated that the fiscal correction would be continued further in 1992-93 and that the fiscal imbalance would be reduced by restricting expenditure.

(c) In submitting the budget for 1993-94, the then Finance Minister, Shri Manmohan Singh stated (paragraphs 8 & 9) as follows:

"Nevertheless, there in no room for complacency. Fiscal imbalances are still large. The efficiency and resource generating capacity of public sector enterprises are still very inadequate. Inflationary expectations have not yet been purged from the system and inflationary pressure could easily build up again if fiscal discipline is relaxed. The economy is still vulnerable to external shocks and loss of confidence. The riots and disturbances in December and January have also taken their toll, by disrupting domestic production and exports and by casting doubts about the stability of our polity and society and our determination to persevere with the difficult task of economic reform. We can ill afford such doubts.

The priorities for economic policy, at this critical stage of our economic restructuring are very clear:

- We must continue with the fiscal correction to ensure that inflationary expectations are effectively curbed; to this end, the fiscal deficit both at the Centre and in the States must be further reduced as a percentage of GDP.
- The room for fiscal manoeuvre gained by restraining expenditure over the past two years must be used to give a strong fillip to development expenditure in 1993-94, especially for programmes of poverty alleviation, rural development and the vital social services such as education and health.
- The hesitant industrial recovery must be converted into a strong revival in 1993-94, which can then be followed by a vigorous boom in the last three years of the Eighth Plan.
- We must take further progress with our announced strategy of tax reform, moving to a simpler tax system, with moderate rates and much greater focus on compliance.
- We must ensure that our economic strategy gives full

support to agriculture on which the livelihood and well-being of the majority of our people depend, and also to agro-processing industries, which have a tremendous potential for increasing employment and income in rural areas.

Finally, exports must be made a truly high priority national endeavour so that we can move as quickly as possible to managing the balance of payments without the need for continued exceptional financing from abroad. This is the only meaningful route to self reliance.

The expenditure and tax proposals for 1993-94, which I will be presenting shortly, have been tailored to meet these objectives."

(d) In presenting the budget for 1995-96, Shri Manmohan Singh, the then Finance Minister had observed (paragraphs 5 and 6) as follows:

We have come a long way, but the journey is far from over. We need to redouble our efforts in several areas to consolidate our gains, and push the economy to even better performance. This is both feasible and also necessary to achieve our goals. Reforms in the areas of taxation, trade and industrial policies and the financial sector have yielded good results. They need to be completed as planned, so as to enhance the efficiency and competitiveness of our economy. Barriers to further expansion of agriculture have to be identified and lifted. The public sector has to be revamped. Industrial relations have to provide for greater flexibility in deployment of labour. Delivery systems for social services have to be modernised, plugging loopholes and promoting cost effectiveness. Capital market reforms have to be widened and deepened to strengthen investor protection. Insurance sector reforms have to be pursued with the aim of greatly widening access to insurance services and promoting competitive and efficient customer-oriented services. We must and will push ahead in all these areas.

There are also some weak spots, which have surfaced and need to be addressed urgently. After the initial successes in fiscal consolidation, further progress has proved much more difficult. The fiscal deficit increased sharply in 1993-94 and the pressure on the deficit has continued in 1994-95. These developments must be countered through determined action. If we try to fund every project and programme irrespective of the revenues available, we only generate high inflation, high interest rates which choke off investment, and a proliferation of under-funded, incomplete projects. This approach will only jeopardise our basic objective of development with social justice since it is the poor who will suffer most from the resultant inflation and slow growth of employment opportunities. We must, therefore, ensure that fiscal discipline is further improved in the years ahead.

(e) The Economic Survey for 1995-96 observed as follows (paragraphs 1 to 5):

"Further consolidation of fiscal balance, tax reform, social equity and poverty alleviation were some of the major considerations for the 1995-96 budget of the Central Government. The fiscal setback of 1993-94 is likely to be fully recovered in 1995-96. Over the five years period 1990-91 to 1995-96 (BE) the fiscal deficit is estimated to decline by 2.8 per cent of GDP. The contribution of the decline in Plan expenditure (0.7 per cent of GDP) is less than 2/7th the contribution of the decline in non-plan expenditure (2.6 per cent of GDP). The primary deficit, which is a better measure of the effort made, declined by 3.8 per cent of GDP over the period.

Gross dissaving by the Central Government which rose sharply in 1993-94 and then declined in 1994-95 (RE), is estimated to decline still further to 1.7 per cent of GDP in 1995-96 (BE). Total outstanding liabilities of the Central Government, after reaching a peak of 69.7 per cent of GDP in 1993-94 are on the decline. A substantial proportion of these liabilities are on behalf of the States, Union Territories and Public Sector Enterprises. Loans given to them constituted over 31 per cent of the total marketable outstanding liabilities, arrived after excluding borrowings from RBI, in 1994-95 (RE). The book value of the economic assets aggregate to another 26 per cent of these liabilities.

Thus, only 43 per cent of the marketable outstanding liabilities are on account of social and administrative assets and expenditure.

The outlay for the Annual Plan 1995-96 for the Centre, States and Union Territories is estimated to increase by 21.1 per cent compared to the outlay in 1994-95 (RE). Financial performance of the Departmental Commercial Undertakings is estimated to improve in 1995-96 (BE). Postal deficit is estimated to decline from Rs. 352 crores in 1994-95 (RE) to Rs. 304 crores in 1995-96 (BE).

Reforms in the tax system has been one of the key elements of the structural reforms initiated since July 1991. These reforms have encompassed both direct and indirect taxes and have moved towards a tax structure which is simple, relies on moderate tax rates with a wider base and better enforcement and serves the objectives of equity and efficiency. Substantial progress has been made in the last five years. The maximum marginal rate of personal income tax was reduced from 56 per cent to 40 per cent and exemption limit raised from Rs. 22,000 in 1991 to Rs. 40,000 in 1995. The rates of corporate income tax, (inclusive of 15 per cent surcharge) which were 51.75 per cent for publicly held company and 57.5 per cent for closely held company were unified and reduced to 46 per cent. In the case of foreign companies the tax rate was brought down from 65 to 55 per cent. Peak import duty rates, which were in excess of 300 per cent prior to reforms were brought down in a phased manner to 50 per cent. Excise duty regime has been greatly improved with a significant switchover from specific to *ad valorem* duties to ensure built-in revenue elasticity and a far reaching rationalisation of the rate structure. The ambit of MODVAT i.e., credit for taxes paid on inputs, was extended to cover capital goods, R&D equipment, POL etc. The number of *ad valorem* excise duty rates were brought down to 10 (including nil rate) and a large number of end use exemptions eliminated. The budget for 1995-96 continued the emphasis on strengthening the incentives for investment, simplification, lower rates and greater buoyancy. To facilitate expansion of quality infrastructure a five-year tax holiday was provided to enterprises which provide certain facilities in the area of highways, bridges, etc.

Overall, tax reforms since July 1991 have helped in correcting the imbalance in the structure of revenue sources. Direct taxation is generally regarded a more equitable way of raising revenue. It is noteworthy that the share of direct taxes in GDP rose from 2.1 per cent in 1990-91 to an estimated 2.9 per cent in 1995-96".

(f) The Economic Survey for 1998-99 observed as follows (paragraphs 74 to 80):

"The most intractable and long standing issue confronting us is that of the fiscal prudence. The various aspects of the fiscal problem, namely the fiscal deficit, the revenue deficit, unproductive expenditures and unsustainable subsidies are now fairly well known. With the exception of the initial success achieved in 1991-92 under the pressure of the balance of payments crisis, subsequent improvements have alternated with setbacks and reversal. As a result, the position today is not significantly better than in 1991-92. There is therefore a clear need for building a political consensus on this issue in terms of both constitutional and administrative measures that need to be taken.

The fiscal deficit is the key parameter of macroeconomic policy, which has profound implications for inflation, interest rates, investment, growth, the financial system, balance of payments and last, but by no means least, overall credibility of Government's macroeconomic policy. For the Central Government the fiscal deficit simply reflects the net borrowing requirement of the Government. A high fiscal deficit leads to excess borrowing from either the RBI or the market for loanable funds. Excessive borrowing from the RBI leads to high monetary growth, which fuels inflation and puts pressure on the exchange rate. When considering Government borrowing from the market, the fiscal deficits of the Centre and State Governments need to be aggregated [in 1997-98 (R.E.) this was 7.4 per cent of GDP]. Such a high level of Government borrowing pre-empts funds which could otherwise have been used productively in industry, agriculture and services. High deficits also keep interest rates high and investment and growth low. Excess Government borrowing also places undue pressure on the domestic financial system and capital markets. There is also the long-term issue of sustainability of fiscal deficit.

Long term fiscal sustainability generally requires bringing down the primary deficit (gross fiscal deficit minus interest payments) to below zero. For the Centre and States together, the primary deficit is estimated at 2.4 per cent of GDP in 1997-98 (RE), with little prospect of improvement in 1998-99. A reduction in the primary deficit to zero would, therefore, require at least a 2.4 per cent of GDP reduction in the fiscal deficit. If the entire adjustment falls on the Central Government, this would require a reduction of the Central fiscal deficit to about 3.3 per cent of GDP. This target assumes that the real interest rate in the economy is lower than the growth rate. If this condition does not hold for any reason, a primary surplus and consequently a greater reduction in the fiscal deficit would be required.

Quite clearly, fiscal consolidation is absolutely necessary for containing inflation, reducing interest rates, promoting investment and growth, and fostering reasonable stability in the financial system and the foreign exchange market. Experience from the rest of the world underlines the importance of fiscal deficit reduction in regard to reducing interest rates and inflation. It is therefore essential to put the fiscal deficit on an irreversible and unambiguously declining trend.

In a broader qualitative sense, sustainability also depends on the quality of the government expenditure and the nature of the tax system underpinning the fiscal system. Concern about the revenue deficit stems from the legitimate concern that a significant part of revenue expenditures are of low priority. These low priority expenditures and non-targeted subsidies need to be identified and eliminated. This is also essential for freeing up funds for completing the unfinished tasks of universal primary education, effective public health systems and modern water and sewage systems for the entire population. The impact of the Fifth Pay Commission and its aftermath on revenue deficits of Centre, States and local bodies lends urgency to the need to downsize government. The time has perhaps come to reconsider the issue of constitutional limits on the deficit as well as to take up the challenge of reengineering government.

The task of reforming the tax system must also be carried forward and completed. But such reforms must be accompanied by determined efforts to augment revenue mobilisation through base broadening, improved administration and other means. The decline in the tax to GDP ratio of recent years must be reversed.

The commendable but gargantuan task of decontrol and de-bureaucratisation which every government in the nineties has set for itself remains unfinished. The extent and depth of the economic distortions such controls have created are perhaps still not fully appreciated by all, even though the negative effect on the public is known to all who interact with the government. The remaining price and distribution controls must be eliminated. At the State level this must be preceded by a major effort to identify such controls. Investment controls are the second most pernicious legacy of the control era and remain in several infrastructure service sectors. SSI reservation is another form of investment control. The need to replace all quantitative restrictions by fiscal measures was recognised even in the eighties, yet import and export controls remain widespread in certain sectors like agriculture. Though reform of the foreign exchange system has been one of the prominent areas of reform, the operation of exchange controls still requires improvement, particularly for exporters and knowledge-based industries. Similarly, though some of the well-known financial sector controls have been removed, many controls remain embedded in the laws, rules, regulations, norms and procedures".

55.2.1 For reducing consumption expenditure it is necessary to:

(i) cut down expenditure on subsidies (whether direct or indirect),

(ii) reduce interest burden by restricting its borrowings only to the extent necessary for investments in durable assets which are productive or reduce recurring liabilities, and are needed for the planned development process the country has undertaken,

(iii) stop all non-essential expenditure and make the delivery system efficient, honest and sensitive to the needs of development.

(iv) make the public sector and departmental undertakings cost-effective, efficient and profitable.

55.2.2 The growth of expenditure of the Central Government on subsidy has been discussed in paragraphs 27.4.4, 27.4.5 and 27.4.6. In the recent years, subsidies have accounted for 9 to 16 per cent of the total revenue expenditure of the Central Government. It should be possible to abolish all forms of subsidies, except in rare cases e.g. subsidised food articles only to the people below poverty line.

55.2.3 In the recent years, the expenditure of the Central Government on interest was 19 to 34 per cent of its total revenue expenditure due to massive borrowings both from internal and external sources. With a view to reducing expenditure on interest, it is necessary to restrict borrowings only to the extent absolutely essential for planned development, that too mainly for investment in such durable assets, from which the returns will be adequate not only to meet repayment liabilities (with interest on the borrowed funds) but also to make net addition to revenue. Use of borrowed funds for meeting revenue deficits would also stop when it is possible to remove the revenue deficits by correcting the fiscal imbalances.

55.2.4 It is necessary to examine and prune all non-essential expenditure. Till fiscal balance is restored by removing revenue deficit, it is absolutely essential that even expenditure on some apparent populist measures is curtailed or stopped at least for the time being. For example, the employment programmes now in vogue mostly do not produce any durable productive asset. As a temporary emergency relief measures consequent on a natural calamity, such an employment programme may be unavoidable. But as a long term measure such a programme is difficult to sustain without causing imbalance to the fiscal system, when there is no return flow to the budget.

Besides, there are leakages in such a programme as a result of which only a small portion of the intended benefit reaches the needy people for the benefit of whom such a programme is meant. In other words, there is lot of wastage in such a programme. Even in the bankable schemes for the rural poor, subsidised by Government, full benefit does not reach the target group because of leakages which are, in effect, wastages in the intermediate stages, mainly in banks.

An indepth enquiry may disclose how the intermediaries, including some of those in banks, take away a substantial portion of the intended benefit and how little really reaches the target group.

56.1 The public sector undertakings have not been giving adequate return to the budget commensurate with the massive investment made in them. There is no denying the fact that the public sectors have to play an important role in the national economy. But they have to function efficiently and make adequate contribution to the budget in return of the investments made in them. Many of the public sector undertakings, however, suffer due to inefficiency in other sectors, e.g. shortage of power, delays in transportation of raw materials, etc. Disinvestment is not the panacea for all the ills in public sector units. Disinvestment may be the soft option for Government to have some additional resources, but would certainly not make the public sector units cost-effective and efficient for generating not only resources for themselves, but also for contributing adequate return on investments in them.

56.2 The tax base has to be broadened by making the rich, including those who are rich in agricultural income, to pay more on their income and conspicuous consumption (in the form of expenditure tax).

56.3 In addition to the fiscal imbalance the country is facing, there is another serious problem. We are now facing side by side rising inflation with a high level of unemployment. In his book "*The Great Depression of 1990*", Dr. Ravi Batra has made the following observations in respect of such a situation:

"This problem eluded Keynes, for there is supposed to be a trade off between unemployment and inflation in the Keynesian system; both cannot rise or decline at the same time. As yet there is no consensus among economists– there hardly ever is – as to how the new challenge should be met. The problem admits of no simple, and politically feasible, solution."

Dr. Batra has added "........... in 1973 the world economy was jolted by an international cartel called Organisation of Petroleum Exporting Countries (OPEC). There was four-fold rise in oil prices as a result, and the U.S. economy tottered once again. The recession of 1973-75 was the steepest since the Great Crash, but more than that, it was accompanied by unprecedented double digit inflation. Keynesian remedies were applied once again and as a consequence the economy recovered, only to be hit by another bout of stagnation lasting from 1980 to 1982. Since then both inflation and unemployment have declined, but as no fundamental reform has been undertaken, the crisis is still simmering, ready to erupt again at any moment".

The above observations are no less applicable to our country. In fact, in our country the crisis of togetherness of both inflation and huge unemployment has been becoming deeper and deeper. While the soft option of the populist programmes of employment have not been of adequate and lasting help to the target group of people, as mentioned earlier, they have contributed substantially to the fiscal imbalance which the country has been facing.

It is now for our economists and planners to give serious thought to this problem; so far as generation of employment is concerned, this will have to be through investment in gainful activities only and not through populist measures mentioned earlier. The economists and planners will also have to determine to what extent the money supply will have to be restricted by curtailing overall budgetary deficit, without, of course, decelerating the planning process. All these need hard decisions.

56.4 It has been mentioned that not only the reasons for the fiscal imbalances in the centre but also their possible solutions, which needed hard decisions, were already known to Government. One of these is cutting down expenditure (whether implicit or explicit) on subsidies. This was emphasised in the Economic Survey for 1984-85 placed in the Parliament in the early part of 1986 by the then Finance Minister a few days before placing the budget for 1985-86. In the Economic Survey for the subsequent years also apprehensions had been expressed about the effect of continuous increase in subsidies.

It was, however, noticed that the proposal for abolition of subsidy on fertilizer in the budget for 1991-92 had generated lot of opposition in Parliament, with the harassed Finance Minister at the receiving end from all sides including his own. Subsidy on fertilizer in 1991-92 was merely Rs. 5185 crores. As compared to this, in 1997-98 (B.E), subsidy on fertilizer increased by 120 per cent to Rs. 11,388 crores, despite the fact that the country had already reached the peak of green revolution much earlier. This is the fate of one hard decision contemplated half a decade earlier and intended to be implemented in the budget for 1991-92, although the farmers get compensated for any increase in cost of agricultural products by enhanced prices fixed by the Agricultural Prices Commission from time to time. Thus, it is the ultimate consumers of the agricultural products who would pay for the increase in prices of fertilizers. Presumably, similar would have been the fate of the proposal for abolition of subsidy for promotion of export had that not been more than counter-balanced by liberalisation of foreign trade and industrial policy.

In the above context the following questions arise:

(i) Was it in the national interest to allege a linkage of this proposed cutting down of subsidies with the contemplated loan from the International Monetary Fund, when the need for the same was emphasised much earlier in the Economic Survey for 1984-85?

(ii) Will any Finance Minister be able to take any hard decision to pull the country out of the fiscal imbalances, if any purely economic decision needed for the same is over-shadowed by merely political consideration?

56.5 The instance in paragraph 56.3 is only an illustration. Over the past several years, Finance Ministers had told us that the days of soft option were over and that hard decisions were necessary. There is no sign of any really hard decisions for correcting the fiscal imbalance. The fiscal imbalance has, therefore, been continuing. It is high time for the politicians of our country to rise above petty considerations relating to self, party and political interests in taking hard economic decisions for restoring the fiscal health of the nation.

Our politicians, economists and intellectuals of all hues and thinking should ponder about this seriously not only to take the Country out of the financial crisis but also to ensure disciplined financial management in the future.

INDEX